Crochet in a Day

42 FAST & FUN PROJECTS

SALENA BACA

WITH DANYEL PINK AND EMILY TRUMAN

STACKPOLE BOOKS

Guilford, Connecticut

Published by Stackpole Books
An imprint of The Rowman & Littlefield Publishing Group, Inc.
4501 Forbes Blvd., Ste. 200
Lanham, MD 20706
www.stackpolebooks.com

Distributed by NATIONAL BOOK NETWORK
800-462-6420

Photography: Emily Truman
Technical Editing: Danyel Pink, Emily Truman
Models: Jamie Johnston, Rachel Johnston, Michaela Truman, Caden Truman, Jesse Price, and Dave Price

British Library Cataloguing in Publication Information available

Library of Congress Cataloging-in-Publication Data
Names: Baca, Salena, author. | Pink, Danyel, author. | Truman, Emily, author.
Title: Crochet in a day : 42 fast & fun projects / Salena Baca with Danyel
   Pink and Emily Truman.
Description: Lanham, MD : Stackpole Books, an imprint of The Rowman &
   Littlefield Publishing Group, Inc., [2019] | Includes index.
Identifiers: LCCN 2018040408 (print) | LCCN 2018040815 (ebook) | ISBN
   9780811766166 (electronic) | ISBN 9780811737081 (pbk. : alk. paper)
Subjects: LCSH: Crocheting.
Classification: LCC TT825 (ebook) | LCC TT825 .B2936 2019 (print) | DDC
   746.43/4—dc23
LC record available at https://lccn.loc.gov/2018040408

The paper used in this publication meets the minimum requirements of American National Standard for Information Sciences—Permanence of Paper for Printed Library Materials, ANSI/NISO Z39.48-1992.

First Edition

Printed in the United States of America

Contents

Introduction

Crochet designers Salena Baca, Danyel Pink, and Emily Truman share a love for instant gratification when it comes to crochet projects. With easy-to-learn stitch patterns and fast-working stitches, the designs they created for this book are all made to work up quickly, most in just a few hours. Here they each offer a bit of insight into the designs they contributed to *Crochet in a Day*.

Salena Baca

SalenaBacaCrochet.com
My favorite types of crochet projects are ones that look complicated but are actually quick to work up. The pieces I've created for this collection use yarns that are readily sourced, or substituted, and are easy to approach with stunning results. When you're flipping through this awesome collection of crochet designs and styles, you'll see that quick and easy does not mean plain or ordinary!

Danyel Pink

www.DanyelPinkDesigns.com
I'm one of those crafters who suffers from "one-sock syndrome." You know the feeling—when you've finished the first sock and you have trouble forcing yourself to begin the second. I do appreciate the time and effort that go into big projects, but I often find myself drawn to projects that are bright and full of texture, and that work up in a day or two. When designing my pieces for this collection, quick and colorful were my main focus. If those features appeal to you, too, I know you will be delighted with this fantastic pattern collection!

Emily Truman

www.ravelry.com/people/Emilymtruman
The almost instant gratification that comes from a quick crochet project is what got me hooked on the craft. I love to hold a completed project in my hand and feel that sense of pride. Combine this feeling with some gorgeous texture or classic lace, and you have an amazing project that can be completed in about an evening. I took those characteristics for my inspiration and designed a wide variety of projects, from home decor to gorgeous wearables. The entire collection is packed with amazing projects that work up fast and give you finished products of which to be proud!

Additional Resources

Some crochet stitches and techniques are best learned with a video instead of written definitions and text alone. Please visit the American Crochet Association on YouTube (youtube.com/c/AmericanCrochetAssociation) for an assortment of tutorials on crochet basics like the magic ring (adjustable loop), slipknot, invisible join, color changes, and much more!

Hats &

Headbands

Alaskan Dusk Hat

Designed by Emily Truman

During summer in Alaska, the sun doesn't quite set. Dusk is an in-between time with subtle differences in light, as in the texture of this hat.

Skill Level
Intermediate

Sizes/Finished Measurements
Child (Teen, Adult Small, Adult Large)
Circumference: 19 (20, 21, 22) in./48 (51, 53, 56) cm
Height: 8.5 (9, 9.5, 10) in./21.5 (23, 24, 25) cm

Yarn
Knit Picks City Tweed Aran, heavy worsted weight #4 yarn (55% merino wool, 25% superfine alpaca, 20% Donegal tweed; 164 yd./150 m per 3.5 oz./100 g skein)
- 1 (1, 2, 2) skeins Jacquard 24524

Hook & Other Materials
- US Size H-8 (5.0 mm) crochet hook
- 1 button (optional)
- Yarn needle

Gauge
16 sts in pattern and 10 rows = 4 in./10 cm
Adjust hook size if necessary to obtain gauge.

Special Stitch
3rd loop = Skip front and back top loops and work sts into 3rd loop of hdc behind front and back loops. When working in turned rows, the 3rd loop is in front of work.

Notes
- Body is worked in rows, and then seamed. Brim is added and worked in rounds. Crown is also worked in rows and cinched closed.
- Pattern is written for Child size, with adjustments for larger sizes in parentheses.
- Beginning ch-1 does not count as a st.

Instructions

Body

Ch 21 (25, 29, 33).

Row 1: Working in back bump of ch, hdc in 2nd ch from hook and in each ch across, turn—20 (24, 28, 32) hdc.

Row 2: Ch 1, *3rd loop hdc in next, FLO hdc in next, BLO hdc in next, FLO hdc in next; repeat from * across, turn—20 (24, 28, 32) hdc.

Row 3: Ch 1, *BLO hdc in next, FLO hdc in next, 3rd loop hdc in next, FLO hdc in next; repeat from * across, turn—20 (24, 28, 32) hdc.

Repeat Rows 2–3 until length measures 19 (20, 21, 22) in./48 (51, 53, 56) cm.

Align Row 1 and last row with RS together and sl st through both layers in each st across. Fasten off.

Crown

Join yarn with sl st in any st of crown (RS), sc2tog in each row end around; without joining, continue to sc2tog in each st around, working in a spiral until approx. 6–12 sts remain. Fasten off, leaving a long tail. With yarn needle and remaining tail, weave tail through each remaining st. Pull tight to cinch. Fasten off securely and weave in ends. Turn hat so seam is facing inward.

Brim

Round 1 (RS): Attach yarn to bottom of hat with a sl st, ch 1, sc in each row end around, do not join.

Rounds 2–6 (6, 7, 7): BLO sc in each st around.

After last round, sl st in next st.

Fasten off and weave in ends.

Amelia Ear Warmer

Designed by Danyel Pink

An ear warmer is an excellent alternative to a hat on chilly days. This project has a great, thick texture, and the trim offers a fun pop of color!

Skill Level
Easy

Sizes/Finished Measurements
One size fits most teens/women.
Length is adjustable.
Height: 4.25 in./11 cm

Yarn

Lion Brand Vanna's Choice, worsted weight #4 yarn (100% acrylic; 170 yd./156 m per 3.5 oz./100 g skein)
- 1 skein Fern 171 (Color A)
- 1 skein Linen 099 (Color B)

Hook & Other Materials
- US Size I-9 (5.5 mm) crochet hook
- Yarn needle

Gauge
6 sts and 6 rows = 2 in./5 cm
Gauge is not critical. Add/subtract rows as needed to adjust size.

Notes
- Ch-1 at beginning of a row or round does not count as a st.
- To "join with a sc," put yarn on hook, insert hook into indicated st and pull up loop, yo and pull through both loops on hook to complete sc.

Instructions

With Color A, ch 12.

Row 1: (Sc, dc) in 2nd ch from hook, *skip 1 ch, (sc, dc) in next; repeat from * across to last 2 chs, skip 1 ch, sc in last ch, ch 1, turn—11 sts.

Row 2: [(Sc, dc) in sc, skip next dc] 5 times, sc in last sc, ch 1, turn—11 sts.

Repeat Row 2 until piece measures 1.5 to 2 in./4 to 5 cm smaller than head circumference.

With RS together, join piece end-to-end and sl st evenly through both layers to form circle. Fasten off Color A.

Trim

Turn ear warmer right-side-out (seam on inside).

Working into ends of rows, join Color B with a sc in any "gap" on side of ear warmer near seam, dc in same gap, (sc, dc) into each gap around side of ear warmer, join with sl st to 1st sc. Fasten off.

Repeat on other side.

Weave in all ends.

City Tweed Slouch

Designed by Emily Truman

Tweed yarns give an amazing rustic, yet refined, feel to this cozy slouch.

Skill Level
Intermediate

Sizes/Finished Measurements
Small (Medium, Large)
Circumference: 20 (21, 22) in./51 (53, 56) cm
Height: 8.5 (9, 10) in./21.5 (23, 25) cm

Yarn

Knit Picks City Tweed DK, light weight #3 yarn (55% merino wool, 25% superfine alpaca, 20% Donegal tweed; 123 yd./112 m per 1.8 oz./51 g ball)
- 1 ball Tahitian Pearl 24549 (Color A)
- 1 ball Cobalt 25520 (Color B)
- 1 ball Coastal 25521 (Color C)

Hooks & Other Materials
- US Size G-6 (4.0 mm) crochet hook
- US Size H-8 (5.0 mm) crochet hook
- 1 button (1 in./2.5 cm)
- Yarn needle

Gauge
With G-6 hook, 16 hdc = 4 in./10 cm and 5 rounds = 1.25 in./3.2 cm
With H-8 hook, [sc3tog, ch-1] 8 times and 14 rounds = 4 in./10 cm
Adjust hook size if necessary to obtain gauge.

Special Stitches
fhdc (foundation half double crochet) = Ch 2, yo and insert hook in 2nd ch from hook, yo and pull up a loop, yo and pull through 1 loop on hook (*1st ch made*), yo and pull through all loops on hook (*hdc made*), *yo and insert hook into ch of previous foundation st, yo and pull up a loop, yo and pull through 1 loop on hook (*ch made*), yo and pull through all loops on hook (*hdc made*); repeat from * until desired number of fhdc have been made.

3rd loop hdc (3rd loop half double crochet) = Yo and insert hook through 3rd loop (horizontal loop behind front and back loops), yo and pull through all loops on hook.

sc3tog (single crochet 3 stitches together) = [Insert hook in next st, yo and pull up a loop] 3 times, yo and pull through all loops on hook.

Notes

- Hat is worked from the bottom up in joined rounds. Join and turn after each round of Body, as directed. When working in this manner, the 1st st of the new round will be the sl st from the previous round. Always skip the sl st, and begin round in next st.
- Beginning ch-1 does not count as a st. When instructed to join, sl st to 1st st of round.
- Keep a loose tension throughout.
- Carry unused yarn to WS of hat.
- Pattern is written for size Small with adjustments for larger sizes in parentheses.

Instructions

Brim

With G-6 hook and Color A:

Round 1 (RS): 70 (80, 90) fhdc, join—70 (80, 90) hdc.

Rounds 2–5: Ch 1, 3rd loop hdc in each st around, join—70 (80, 90) hdc.

Join last round with Color B.

Body

With H-8 hook and Color B:

Round 1 (RS): Ch 1, sc3tog over next 3 sts beginning in same st, ch 1, *sc3tog beginning in last leg of previous st and in next 2 sts, ch 1; repeat from * around, last leg of last st will be completed in 1st st of round, join, turn—70 (80, 90) sts.

Round 2: With Color C, ch 1, sc3tog over next 3 sts beginning in same st, ch 1, *sc3tog beginning in last leg of previous st and in next 2 sts, ch 1; repeat from * around, last leg of last st will be completed in 1st st of round, join, turn—70 (80, 90) sts.

Repeat Round 2, alternating Colors A, B, and C until height measures 8 (8.5, 9.5) in./20 (21.5, 24) cm or as desired for beanie or slouchy.

Crown

With H-8 hook and continuing color pattern:

Rounds 1–4: Ch 1, sc3tog over next 3 sts beginning in same st, ch 1, *sc3tog over next 3 sts beginning in next st, ch 1; repeat from * around, if 1 or 2 sts remain (sc, ch 1) in remaining sts, join, turn.

Finishing

Fasten off, leaving a long tail, and weave through remaining sts. Pull tight to close and secure.

Weave in all ends.

Attach a button to cover Brim seam.

Flower Motif Slouch

Designed by Emily Truman

M otif slouches are one of my favorite projects to make. They add a light, flowery feel with basic stitches.

Skill Level
Intermediate

Sizes/Finished Measurements
Teen/Adult Small (Adult Large)
Circumference: 20 (22) in./51 (56) cm
Height: 8 (9) in./20 (25) cm

Yarn

Knit Picks Chroma Worsted, medium weight #4 yarn (70% wool, 30% nylon; 198 yd./181 m per 3.5 oz./100 g skein)
• 1 skein Lupine 26471 (Color A)
• 1 skein Avalon 26552 (Color B)

Hook & Other Materials
• US Size H-8 (5.0 mm) crochet hook
• Yarn needle
• Stitch marker

Gauge
After Round 6, motif should measure 6.5 in./16.5 cm in diameter
Adjust hook size if necessary to obtain gauge.

Special Stitches
2-dc Cl (2 double crochet cluster) = [Yo and insert hook in designated st or space, yo and pull up loop, yo and pull through 2 loops] twice in same st, yo and pull through all loops on hook.
hdc2tog (half double crochet 2 stitches together) = Yo and insert hook into st, yo and pull up loop, yo and insert hook into next st, yo and pull up loop, yo and pull through all loops on hook.

Note
• Beginning ch-1 or ch-2 does not count as a st.

Instructions

Motif (all sizes)

With Color A, make magic ring (see "Additional Resources" on page vii for link to video tutorial).

Round 1: Ch 2, dc in ring (*counts as 2-dc Cl*) ch 2, [2-dc Cl in ring, ch 2] 7 times, sl st to 1st dc to join—8 Cl, 8 ch-2 spaces.

Round 2: Sl st in 1st ch-2 space, ch 1, sc in same space, ch 4, *sc in next ch-2 space, ch 4; repeat from * around, sl st to 1st sc to join—8 ch-4 spaces.

Round 3: *Sl st in next ch-4 space, (ch 3, 2-dc Cl, ch 2, 2-dc Cl, ch 3, sl st) in same space; repeat from * around, sl st in 1st ch of beginning ch-3, sl st in 2nd and 3rd chs, sl st in top of cluster—8 petals.

Round 4: Sl st in ch-2 space, *ch 8, sl st in next ch-2 space; repeat from * around, working last sl st in 1st sl st of round to join—8 ch-8 spaces.

Round 5: Sl st in ch-8 space, ch 1, (4 sc, ch 2, 4 sc) in each ch-8 space around, sl st to 1st sc to join—64 sc + 8 ch-2 spaces.

Round 6: Ch 8 (*counts as dc, ch-5*), *sc in next ch-2 space, ch 5, skip 4 sc, dc in space between next 2 sc, ch 5; repeat from * around, sl st to 3rd ch of beginning ch-8 to join—8 dc, 8 sc, 16 ch-5 spaces.

Fasten off Color A. Continue with Color B to desired size.

Gauge check: Motif should measure 6.5 in./16.5 cm in diameter.

Teen/Adult Small Only

Round 7: Ch 1, *7 hdc in next ch-5 space, 6 hdc in next ch-5 space; repeat from * around, join—104 hdc.

Rounds 8–15: Ch 1, hdc in each st around, join—104 hdc.

Round 16: Ch 1, *hdc in next 11, hdc2tog; repeat from * around, join—96 hdc.

Round 17: Ch 1, *hdc in next 10, hdc2tog; repeat from * around, join—88 hdc.

Round 18: Ch 1, *hdc in next 9, hdc2tog; repeat from * around, join—80 hdc.

Round 19: Ch 1, *hdc in next 8, hdc2tog; repeat from * around, join—72 hdc.

Round 20: Ch 1, BLO sc in each st around, do not join—72 sc.

Begin working in a spiral and use a st marker to note beginning of each round.

Rounds 21–23: BLO sc in each st around—72 sc.

After last Round, sl st in next st and fasten off. Weave in ends.

Adult Large Only

Round 7: Ch 1, 7 hdc in each ch-5 space around, join—112 hdc.

Rounds 8–17: Ch 1, hdc in each st around, join—112 hdc.

Round 18: Ch 1, *hdc in next 12, hdc2tog; repeat from * around, join—104 hdc.

Round 19: Ch 1, *hdc in next 11, hdc2tog; repeat from * around, join—96 hdc.

Round 20: Ch 1, *hdc in next 10, hdc2tog; repeat from * around, join—88 hdc.

Round 21: Ch 1, *hdc in next 9, hdc2tog; repeat from * around, join—80 hdc.

Round 22: Ch 1, BLO sc in each st around, do not join—80 sc.

Begin working in a spiral and use a st marker to note beginning of each round.

Rounds 23–25: BLO sc in each st around—80 sc.

After last round, sl st in next st and fasten off. Weave in ends.

Hannah Hood

Designed by Danyel Pink

Looking for headwear that won't mess up your hair? This oversize hood sits loosely on your head while providing warmth and protecting your ears from chilly weather.

Skill Level
Intermediate

Sizes/Finished Measurements
One size fits most teens/women.
Measured flat:
Front edge: 15 in./38 cm
Back seam: 10 in./25 cm
Depth: 10.5 in./27 cm

Yarn

Scheepjes Stone Washed XL, bulky weight #5 yarn (70% cotton, 30% acrylic; 82 yd./75 m per 1.76 oz./50 g skein)
• 2 skeins Corundum 848

Hook & Other Materials
• US Size J-10 (6.0 mm) crochet hook
• Yarn needle

Gauge
6 (Cl, ch-1) groups and 8 rows = 4 in./10 cm in pattern stitch
Adjust hook size if necessary to obtain gauge.

Special Stitch
Cl (cluster) = Yo, insert hook in indicated st, yo and pull up loop, yo and draw through 2 loops, yo, insert hook in same st, yo and pull up loop, yo and draw through all 4 loops on hook.

Note
• Ch-1 at beginning of a row does not count as a st.

Instructions

Ch 28 loosely.

Row 1 (RS): Hdc in 2nd ch from hook and in next 25, 3 hdc in last ch, hdc in next 26 on opposite side of starting chain—55 hdc.

Row 2: Ch 1, turn, 2 hdc in 1st st, *ch 1, skip next st, Cl in next; repeat from * across to last 2 sts, ch 1, skip next st, 2 hdc in last—26 Cl, 27 ch-1 spaces, 4 hdc.

Row 3: Ch 1, turn, 2 hdc in 1st st, ch 1, skip next st, *Cl in next ch-1 space, ch 1; repeat from * across to last 2 sts, skip next st, 2 hdc in last—27 Cl, 28 ch-1 spaces, 4 hdc.

Rows 4–20: Repeat Row 3—stitch count increases by 1 Cl and 1 ch-1 space each row—44 Cl, 45 ch-1 spaces, 4 hdc.

Row 21: Ch 1, turn, hdc in 1st st, ch 1, skip next st, *Cl in next ch-1 space, ch 1; repeat from * across to last 2 sts, skip next st, hdc in last—45 Cl, 46 ch-1 spaces, 2 hdc.

Fasten off and weave in ends.

Top Braid

Cut six 13 in./33 cm lengths of yarn. Thread strands through top point of hood. Separate into 3 equal groups and braid. Knot braid end and trim fringe evenly.

Side Braids

Cut six 36 in./91 cm lengths of yarn. Thread strands through ch-1 space at front corner of hood. Separate into 3 equal groups and braid. Knot braid end and trim fringe evenly.

Repeat for second braid.

Heather Convertible Hat/Cowl

Designed by Danyel Pink

This striped slouch also doubles as a cozy cowl. The crown of the hat is cinched with a drawstring so you can easily transform it to suit your mood.

Skill Level
Intermediate

Sizes/Finished Measurements
Adult Small (Adult Large)
Fits 21–22 (23–24) in./53–56 (58–61) cm head circumference

Yarn

Cloudborn Superwash Merino Worsted Twist, light worsted weight #4 yarn
(100% superwash merino wool; 220 yd./201 m per 3.5 oz./100 g hank)
- 1 hank Stone Heather 003 (Color A)
- 1 hank Shaela Heather 107 (Color B)
- 1 hank Ivory 008 (or Ecru) (Color C)

Hooks & Other Materials
- US Size H-8 (5.0 mm) crochet hook
- US Size I-9 (5.5 mm) crochet hook
- Yarn needle

Gauge
10 sc and 14 rows with H-8 hook = 4 in./10 cm
Adjust hook size if necessary to obtain gauge for Band. Gauge for Body is slightly larger and not critical. Measurements provided within pattern.

Notes
- Pattern is written in two sections: the Band is worked in rows, and then the Body is worked in rounds.
- Ch-1 at the beginning of a row/round does not count as a st.
- Do not fasten off at each color change of Body; carry unused colors along inside of hat (see "Additional Resources" on page vii for link to video tutorial).
- Pattern is written for size Adult Small with adjustments for Adult Large in parentheses.

Instructions

Band

With H-8 hook and Color A, ch 9.

Row 1: Sc in 2nd ch from hook and in each ch across, turn—8 sc.

Row 2: Ch 1, sc in 1st st, sc in BL of next 6, sc in last, turn—8 sc.

Rows 3–66 (70): Repeat Row 2.

Band should measure approx. 16 (17.5) in./40.5 (44.5) cm long, unstretched.

Join end-to-end, ch 1, sl st last row to starting ch to form Band.

Do not fasten off. Turn seam to inside. Continue to Body.

Body

Switch to I-9 hook and begin working in rounds.

Round 1: Ch 1, (sc, ch 1, sc) into end of every other row end around, join with sl st to 1st sc—66 (70) sc, 33 (35) ch-1 spaces.

Round 2: With Color B, ch 1, sl st in BL of 1st sc, ch 1, 2 hdc in ch-1 space, skip next sc, *sl st in BL of next sc, ch 1, 2 hdc in next ch-1 space, skip next sc; repeat from * around, join with sl st to 1st ch-1 space—66 (70) hdc, 33 (35) ch-1 spaces.

Round 3: With Color C, ch 1, (hdc, ch 1, hdc) in same ch-1 space, skip 2 hdc, *(hdc, ch 1, hdc) in next ch-1 space, skip 2 hdc; repeat from * around, join with sl st to 1st hdc—66 (70) hdc, 33 (35) ch-1 spaces.

Round 4: With Color A, ch 1, sl st in BL of 1st hdc, ch 1, 2 hdc in ch-1 space, skip next hdc, *sl st in BL of next hdc, ch 1, 2 hdc in next ch-1 space, skip next hdc; repeat from * around, join with sl st to 1st ch-1 space—66 (70) hdc, 33 (35) ch-1 spaces.

Round 5: With Color B, repeat Round 3.

Round 6: With Color C, repeat Round 4.

Rounds 7–26: Repeat Rounds 3 and 4, alternating Colors A, B, and C each round.
Hat should measure approx. 10.5 in./27 cm tall.
Fasten off and weave in all ends.

Drawstring

Holding a strand of each Color A and Color B together, crochet a 24 in./61 cm chain (or longer, if desired).
Cut one 8 in./20 cm strand of each color, loop through first chain, and knot to secure fringe. Repeat on other end of drawstring. Trim ends evenly.

Weave drawstring evenly in and out through ch-1 spaces of Round 26.
Carefully cinch top of hat closed.
Loosen drawstring and tuck Band under to wear as a cowl.

Kaleidoscope Slouch

Designed by Danyel Pink

T his lovely, openwork slouch is a joy to crochet! It is perfect for any season and looks great in any color.

Skill Level
Easy

Sizes/Finished Measurements
Adult Small (Adult Large)
Fits 22 (24) in./56 (61) cm head circumference
Length: 10 in./25 cm

Yarn

Red Heart Unforgettable, worsted weight #4 yarn (100% acrylic;
  270 yd./246 m per 3.5 oz./100 g skein)
  • 1 skein Polo 3956

Hooks & Other Materials
  • US Size H-8 (5.0 mm) crochet hook
  • US Size J-10 (6.0 mm) crochet hook
  • Measuring tape
  • Stitch marker
  • Yarn needle

Gauge
8 sc and 10 rows in BL ribbing with H-8 hook = 2 in./5 cm
Adjust hook size if necessary to obtain gauge.

Notes
  • Beginning ch-1 of each row or round does not count as a st.
  • A ch-3 at the beginning of a round counts as a dc.
  • Pattern is written for size Adult Small with adjustments for larger sizes in parentheses.

Instructions

Band

With H-8 hook, ch 9.

Row 1: Sc in 2nd ch from hook and in each ch across, ch 1, turn—8 sc.

Row 2: Sc in 1st sc, sc in BL of next 6, sc in last sc, ch 1, turn—8 sc.

Rows 3–91 (98): Repeat Row 2.

Join Band end-to-end and sl st through first and last rows to form circle. Do not fasten off. Turn right-side-out.

Body

Switch to J-10 hook. Work Round 1 into ends of rows of Band. Mark beginning of each round with stitch marker.

Round 1 (RS): Ch 3, 2 dc in same st as join, skip 2 sts, sc in next, ch 3, skip 3 sts, *3 dc in next, skip 2 sts, sc in next, ch 3, skip 3 sts; repeat from * around, join with sl st to top of beginning ch-3—39 (42) dc, 13 (14) sc, 13 (14) ch-3 spaces.

Round 2: Ch 1, turn, *sc in next ch-3 space, ch 3, 3 dc in next sc; repeat from * around, join with sl st to 1st sc—39 (42) dc, 13 (14) sc, 13 (14) ch-3 spaces.

Round 3: Ch 3, turn, 2 dc in same sc, sc in next ch-3 space, ch 3, *3 dc in next sc, sc in next ch-3 space, ch 3; repeat from * around, join with sl st to top of beginning ch-3—39 (42) dc, 13 (14) sc, 13 (14) ch-3 spaces.

Rounds 4–16: Repeat Rounds 2–3, ending on a Row 2 repeat.

Round 17: Ch 3, turn, dc in same sc, sc in next ch-3 space, ch 2, *2 dc in next sc, sc in next ch-3 space, ch 2; repeat from * around, join with sl st to top of beginning ch-3—26 (28) dc, 13 (14) sc, 13 (14) ch-2 spaces.

Round 18: Ch 1, turn, *sc in next ch-2 space, ch 2, 2 dc in next sc; repeat from * around, join with sl st to 1st sc—26 (28) dc, 13 (14) sc, 13 (14) ch-2 spaces.

Round 19: Ch 3, turn, sc in next ch-2 space, ch 1, *dc in next sc, sc in next ch-2 space, ch 1; repeat from * around, join with sl st to top of beginning ch-3—13 (14) dc, 13 (14) sc, 13 (14) ch-1 spaces.

Round 20: Ch 1, turn, *sc in next ch-1 space, ch 1, dc in next sc; repeat from * around, join with sl st to 1st sc—13 (14) dc, 13 (14) sc, 13 (14) ch-1 spaces.

Fasten off, leaving a 12 in./30.5 cm tail.

Using yarn needle, weave tail in and out through ch-1 spaces of final round, and then cinch top of hat closed.

Finishing

Weave in all ends.

Optional: Block top of hat to create more slouch and set stitches by wetting Body only and then stretching it over a bowl, plate, or other round object and letting it air dry.

Toasty Tunisian Head Wrap

Designed by Danyel Pink

This head wrap is super thick and cozy to keep your ears warm all winter. The Tunisian stitchwork will fool your friends into thinking it's knit!

Skill Level
Intermediate

Finished Measurements
Fits 22–24 in./56–61 cm head circumference
Length: 21 in./53 cm
Width (at widest point): 4.5 in./11.5 cm

Yarn

Scheepjes Stone Washed XL, bulky weight #5 yarn (70% cotton, 30% acrylic; 82 yd./75 m per 1.76 oz./50 g skein)
• 1 skein Blue Apatite 845

Hook & Other Materials
• US Size I-9 (5.5 mm) Tunisian crochet hook
• 2 buttons (0.5 to 0.75 in./1.25 to 2 cm)
• Yarn needle
• Blocking supplies (optional)

Gauge
7 sts and 9 rows in TKS = 2 in./5 cm
Adjust hook size if necessary to obtain gauge.

Special Stitches
TKS (Tunisian knit stitch) = Insert hook through work from front to back between strands of next vertical bar, yo and pull up loop, leave loop on hook.
TKS2tog (Tunisian knit stitch 2 together) = Insert hook under vertical bar of 1st st and through 2nd st, yo and pull up loop, leave loop on hook.
Basic Return Row = Ch 1, *yo and pull through 2 loops; repeat from * until 1 loop remains on hook. Do not turn. Last loop on hook is 1st st of next row.
M1 (make 1 increase) = Insert hook into space between next 2 sts, yo and pull up loop, leave loop on hook.

Instructions

Ch 9.

Row 1: Insert hook into back bump of 2nd ch from hook, yo and draw up loop, *insert hook into back bump of next ch, yo and draw up loop; repeat from * to end of ch. Work Basic Return Row—9 sts.

Row 2: TKS in each st across. Work Basic Return Row—9 sts.

Row 3: TKS in next, skip 1 st, TKS in next 3, skip 1 st, TKS in last 2. Ch 1, yo and draw through 2 loops, ch 1, [yo and draw through 2 loops] 3 times, ch 1, [yo and draw through 2 loops] twice—7 sts, 2 buttonholes.

Row 4: TKS in each st and buttonhole across. Work Basic Return Row—9 sts.

Rows 5–9: TKS in each st across. Work Basic Return Row—9 sts.

Row 10 (increase): TKS in next 2, M1, TKS in next 3, M1, TKS in last 3. Work Basic Return Row—11 sts.

Rows 11–17: TKS in each st across. Work Basic Return Row—11 sts.

Row 18 (increase): TKS in next 2, M1, TKS in next 5, M1, TKS in last 3. Work Basic Return Row—13 sts.

Rows 19–23: TKS in each st across. Work Basic Return Row—13 sts.

Row 24 (increase): TKS in next 2, M1, TKS in next 7, M1, TKS in last 3. Work Basic Return Row—15 sts.

Rows 25–29: TKS in each st across. Work Basic Return Row—15 sts.

Row 30 (increase): TKS in next 2, M1, TKS in next 9, M1, TKS in last 3. Work Basic Return Row—17 sts.

Rows 31–59: TKS in each st across. Work Basic Return Row—17 sts.

Row 60 (decrease): TKS in next 2, TKS2tog, TKS in next 7, TKS2tog, TKS in last 3. Work Basic Return Row—15 sts.

Rows 61–65: TKS in each st across. Work Basic Return Row—15 sts.

Row 66 (decrease): TKS in next 2, TKS2tog, TKS in next 5, TKS2tog, TKS in last 3. Work Basic Return Row—13 sts.

Rows 67–71: TKS in each st across. Work Basic Return Row—13 sts.

Row 72 (decrease): TKS in next 2, TKS2tog, TKS in next 3, TKS2tog, TKS in last 3. Work Basic Return Row—11 sts.

Rows 73–79: TKS in each st across. Work Basic Return Row—11 sts.

Row 80 (decrease): TKS in next 2, TKS2tog, TKS in next, TKS2tog, TKS in last 3. Work Basic Return Row—9 sts.

Rows 81–89: TKS in each st across. Work Basic Return Row—9 sts.

Row 90: Sc in each st across.

Fasten off and weave in ends.

Finishing

Using yarn and yarn needle, sew 2 buttons to end of head wrap opposite buttonholes. Adjust buttons on head wrap to customize to desired size.

Gently block head wrap to straighten edges or increase length, if desired.

Wraps & Other

Wearables

Chroma Shawl

Designed by Emily Truman

The beautiful, self-striping Knit Picks Chroma takes this delightful shell pattern to a whole new level.

Skill Level
Easy

Size/Finished Measurements
Before blocking:
Width: 9 in./23 cm
Length: 56 in./142 cm

Yarn

Knit Picks Chroma Worsted, worsted weight #4 yarn (70% superwash wool, 30% nylon; 198 yd./181 m per 3.5 oz./100 g skein)
- 2 skeins Carnival 26553

Hook & Other Materials
- US Size I-9 (5.5 mm) crochet hook
- Yarn needle
- Blocking supplies (optional)

Gauge
Gauge is not critical for this project.

Notes
- To adjust width, use a beginning chain in multiples of 8 + 5.
- For a lighter shawl with more drape, increase hook size.

Instructions

Ch 37.

Row 1: Sc in 9th ch from hook, *ch 5, skip 3, sc in next—8 ch-spaces.

Row 2: Ch 3 (*counts as 1st dc, now and throughout*), 2 dc in same, *sc in next ch-5 space, ch 5, sc in next ch-5 space, 5 dc in next sc; repeat from * across to last 2 ch-spaces, sc in next ch-5 space, ch 5, sc in 6th ch of beginning ch-8—4 ch-5 spaces.

Row 3: Ch 3, 2 dc in same, *sc in next ch-5 space, ch 5, sc in 3rd dc of next 5-dc group, 5 dc in next sc; repeat from * across to last ch-5 space, sc in next ch-5 space, ch 5, sc in 3rd ch of beginning ch-3—4 ch-5 spaces.

Row 4: Ch 6, sc in next ch-5 space, *5 dc in next sc, sc in 3rd dc of next 5-dc group, ch 5, sc in next ch-5 space; repeat from * across to last sc, 5 dc in last sc, sc in 3rd ch of beginning ch-3—4 ch-5 spaces.

Row 5: Ch 6, sc in 3rd dc of next 5-dc group, *5 dc in next sc, sc in next ch-5 space, ch 5, sc in 3rd dc of next 5-dc group; repeat from * across to last sc, 5 dc in last sc, sc in 4th ch of beginning ch-6—4 ch-5 spaces.

Row 6: Ch 3, 2 dc in same, *sc in 3rd dc of next 5-dc group, ch 5, sc in next ch-5 space, 5 dc in next sc; repeat from * across to last 5-dc group, sc in 3rd dc of next 5-dc group, ch 5, sc in 4th ch of beginning ch-6—4 ch-5 spaces.

Repeat Rows 3–6 until length measures 56 in./142 cm, or as desired.

Last Row: Ch 1, *3 sc in ch-5 space, skip sc, sc in next 5 dc, skip sc; repeat from * across to last ch-5 space, 3 sc in last ch-5 space, sc in next 2 dc, sc in 3rd ch of beginning ch-3.

Finishing

Fasten off and weave in ends.
Block to rectangular shape if desired.

Diamond Twist Cowl

Designed by Emily Truman

Chroma Twist Bulky adds a new color dimension to the diamonds in this amazing cowl.

Skill Level
Intermediate

Finished Measurements
Circumference: 29 in./73.5 cm
Height: 9 in./23 cm

Yarn

Knit Picks Chroma Twist Bulky, #5 weight yarn (70% superwash wool, 30% nylon; 127 yd./116 m per 3.5 oz./100 g hank)
• 2 hanks Sugar Cookie 27286

Hook & Other Materials
• US Size K-10.5 (6.5 mm) crochet hook
• Yarn needle

Gauge
Gauge is not critical for this project.

Special Stitches
fhdc (foundation half double crochet) = Ch 2, yo and insert hook in 2nd ch from hook, yo and pull up loop, yo and pull through 1 loop on hook (*1st ch made*), yo and pull through all loops on hook (*hdc made*), *yo and insert hook into ch of previous foundation st, yo and pull up loop, yo and pull through 1 loop on hook (*ch made*), yo and pull through all loops on hook (*hdc made*); repeat from * until desired number of fhdc have been made.
shell = (2 dc, ch 1, 2 dc) in indicated st.

Note
• Beginning ch-1 does not count as a st.

Instructions

Round 1: Fhdc 80, sl st to 1st st to form ring.

Round 2: Ch 1, *sc in next, skip 3, ch 5; repeat from * around, sl st to 1st sc to join—20 ch-5 spaces.

Round 3: Ch 3, 2 dc in same (*counts as half-shell*), *sc in ch-5 space, ch 5, sc in next ch-5 space**, shell in next sc; repeat from * around ending last repeat at **, 2 dc in same st as beginning ch-3 (*completes 1st shell*), sl st to 3rd ch of beginning ch-3 to join—10 shells, 10 ch-5 spaces.

Round 4: Ch 1, sc in same, *shell in next sc, sc in next ch-5 space, shell in next sc**, sc in ch-1 space of next shell; repeat from * around ending last repeat at **, sl st to 1st sc to join—20 shells.

Round 5: Ch 3, 2 dc in same (*counts as half-shell*), *sc in ch-1 space of next shell, ch 5, sc in ch-1 space of next shell **, shell in next sc; repeat from * around ending last repeat at **, 2 in same st as beginning ch-3 (*completes 1st shell*), sl st to 3rd ch of beginning ch-3 to join—10 shells, 10 ch-5 spaces.

Round 6: Ch 1, sc in same, *ch 5, sc in next ch-5 space, ch 5**, sc in ch-1 space of next shell; repeat from * around, sl st to 1st sc to join, sl st in next 5 ch—20 ch-5 spaces.

Rounds 7–17: Repeat Rounds 3–6, ending on a repeat of Round 5.

Round 18: Ch 1, sc in same, *ch 4, sc in next ch-5 space, ch 4**, sc in ch-1 space of next shell; repeat from * around ending last repeat at **, sl st to 1st sc to join—20 ch-4 spaces.

Round 19: Ch 1, 4 hdc in each ch-4 space around.

Finishing

Fasten off and weave in ends.

Dreamy Poncho

Designed by Salena Baca

If you've never made a top before, this poncho is very easy to approach. This garment is lightweight, and a great accessory for cooler temperatures for day or evening wear!

Skill Level
Intermediate

Sizes/Finished Measurements
Adult Small (Medium, Large, XL, 1X)
Circumference: 43 (46, 49, 52, 55) in./109 (117, 124.5, 132, 140) cm
Length: 16 (16, 17.75, 17.75, 19.5) in./40.5 (40.5, 45, 45, 49.5) cm

Yarn
Red Heart Yarns Dreamy, medium weight #4 yarn (100% acrylic; 466 yd./426 m per 8.8 oz./250 g skein)
  • 1 skein Grey

Hook & Other Materials
  • US Size K-10.5 (6.5 mm) crochet hook
  • Measuring tape
  • Yarn needle

Gauge
13.5 dc and 5 rows = 4 in./10 cm
Adjust hook size if necessary to obtain gauge.

Notes
  • For best fit, measure around the bust over the arms and work size that is closest to this measurement.
  • Pattern is written for size Adult Small with adjustments for larger sizes in parentheses.
  • Poncho is worked in three sections. Body (lower section) is worked back and forth in rows and then seamed to form a tube. Cowl (upper section) is worked in joined rounds. Border is worked last, into the end rows opposite the neck.
  • A ch-1 or ch-3 at the beginning of a row/round does not count as a st.

Instructions
Body
Ch 52 (52, 58, 58, 64).

Row 1: Dc in 4th ch from hook, dc in next 2, [ch 3, skip 3 sts, dc in next 3] 7 (7, 8, 8, 9) times, ch 3, skip 3 sts, dc in last—49 (49, 55, 55, 61) sts.

Row 2: Ch 3, turn, [3 dc in ch-3 space, ch 3, skip 3 sts] 7 (7, 8, 8, 9) times, 3 dc in next ch-3 space, ch 3, skip 2 sts, dc in last st—49 (49, 55, 55, 61) sts.

Rows 3–52 (56, 60, 64, 68): Repeat Row 2.

Hold first and last rows together, sl st loosely through both layers to form seam. Turn RS out. Do not fasten off—49 (49, 55, 55, 61) sl st.

Neck
Round 1 (RS): Ch 1, 2 sc in each ch-3 space around, sl st to top of 1st sc to join—52 (56, 60, 64, 68) sc.

Rounds 2–5: Ch 1, sc in each st around, sl st to top of 1st sc to join—52 (56, 60, 64, 68) sc.

Fasten off.

Bottom Trim
With RS facing, attach yarn into any ch-3 end row, opposite neck.

Round 1: Ch 1, [3 dc, ch 10, 3 dc] into each ch-3 space around, sl st to top of 1st dc to join—156 (168, 180, 192, 204) dc, 26 (28, 30, 32, 34) ch-10 spaces.

Fasten off.

Finishing
Knot each ch-10 space evenly so that the knot is based close to dc.

Alternative: If you prefer not to knot, add a tassel or pom-pom to each ch-10 space on the border instead of knotting each individually.

Feng Shui Wrap

Designed by Salena Baca

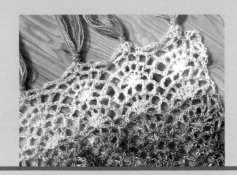

Along wrap is the perfect complement to a simple outfit. Lightweight textured yarn and long color repeats turn these simple stitches into a stunning piece!

Skill Level
Intermediate

Finished Measurements
Width: 66 in./168 cm
Height (without fringe): 10 in./25 cm

Yarn

Lion Brand Shawl in a Ball, medium weight #4 yarn (58% cotton, 39% acrylic, 3% other fiber; 518 yd./473 m per 5.3 oz./150 g skein)
  • 1 skein Feng Shui Grey 207

Hook & Other Materials
  • US Size J-10 (6.0 mm) crochet hook
  • Yarn needle

Gauge
10 sts and 8 rows = 4 in./10 cm
Adjust hook size if necessary to obtain gauge.

Special Stitches
Shell = 5 dc in indicated st.
Fan = (2 dc, ch 3, 2 dc) in indicated st.

Instructions

Ch 232.

Row 1 (RS): Dc in 4th ch from hook (*3 skipped chs do not count as a st*), ch 2, skip 1 ch, sc in next, [ch 2, skip 3 ch, Shell in next, ch 2, skip 3 ch, sc in next, ch 5, skip 3 ch, sc in next] 18 times, ch 2, skip 3 ch, Shell in next, ch 2, skip 3 ch, sc in next, ch 2, skip 1 ch, dc in last, turn—19 Shells, 40 ch-2 spaces, 38 sc.

Row 2: Ch 1 (*not a st*), sc in 1st st, ch 2, [(dc, ch 1) in next 4 dc, dc in next, ch 2, sc in ch-5 space, ch 2] 18 times, (dc, ch 1) in next 4 dc, dc in next, ch 2, sc in last, turn—95 dc, 20 sc.

Row 3: Ch 3 (*not a st*), dc in 1st st, [(dc, ch 2) in next 4 dc, dc in next dc] 19 times, dc in last, turn—97 dc.

Row 4: Ch 3 (*not a st*), dc in 1st st, ch 2, [sc in next ch-2 space, ch 2, skip 1 ch-2 space, Shell in next dc, ch 2, skip 1 ch-2 space, sc in next ch-2 space, ch 5] 18 times, sc in next ch-2 space, ch 2, skip 1 ch-2 space, Shell in next dc, ch 2, skip 1 ch-2 space, sc in next ch-2 space, ch 2, dc in last, turn—19 Shells, 40 ch-2 spaces, 18 ch-5 spaces, 38 sc.

Rows 5–15: Repeat Rows 2–4, ending with a Row 3 repeat.

Row 16: Ch 3 (*not a st*), dc in 1st st, ch 2, [sc in ch-2 space, ch 2, skip 1 ch-2 space, Fan in next dc, ch 2, skip 1 ch-2 space, sc in next ch-2 space, ch 5] 18 times, sc in next ch-2 space, skip 1 ch-2 space, Fan in next dc, ch 2, skip 1 ch-2 space, sc in next ch-2 space, ch 2, dc in last st—19 Fans, 40 ch-2 spaces, 18 ch-5 spaces, 38 sc.

Fasten off and weave in ends.

Fringe

*Cut ten 23 in./58 cm strands of yarn and fold strands in half evenly. With RS facing, using ch-3 space from Row 16, insert center fold of strands from RS to inside of wrap, pull ends through center and secure knot; repeat from * for each ch-3 space across. Trim fringe as desired. After folding and trimming, each fringe bundle should measure approx. 11 in./28 cm in length.

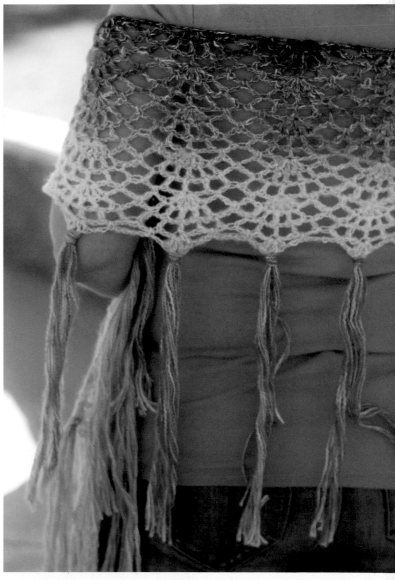

Fringe Vest

Designed by *Salena Baca*

This classic piece can be worn year-round to make your favorite outfit pop!

Skill Level
Intermediate

Sizes/Finished Measurements
Small (Medium, Large, XL, 1X)
Circumference: 20 (25, 30, 35, 40) in./51 (63.5, 76, 89, 101.5) cm
Fits Bust: 30–35 (35–40, 40–45, 45–50, 50–55) in./76–89 (89–101.5, 101.5–114, 114–127, 127–140) cm

Yarn

Red Heart Strata, bulky weight #5 yarn (76% acrylic, 24% nylon; 95 yd./ 86 m per 3.5 oz./100 g skein)
• 2 (2, 3, 3, 3) skeins Teal 2620

Hook & Other Materials
• US Size L-11 (8.0 mm) crochet hook
• Yarn needle

Gauge
10 sts and 8 rows = 4 in./10 cm
Adjust hook size if necessary to obtain gauge.

Notes
• Vest can have up to 4 in./10 cm positive ease and should be open in front. For best fit, measure bust and follow size within range of finished measurements.
• Vest is worked in three parts: Band, Back, Border
• Pattern is written for size Small with adjustments for larger sizes in parentheses.

Instructions

Band

Ch 57 (67, 77, 87, 97).

Row 1 (RS): Dc in 4th ch from hook (*3 skipped chs count as 1st dc*) and in each ch across, turn—55 (65, 75, 85, 95) dc.

Row 2: Ch 4 (*counts as dc, ch-1*), skip 1 st, [dc in next, ch 1, skip 1] 22 (32, 42, 52, 62) times, dc in last, turn—55 (65, 75, 85, 95) sts.

Row 3: Ch 3 (*counts as 1st dc*), dc in each st across, turn—55 (65, 75, 85, 95) dc.

Rows 4–7: Repeat Rows 2–3.

Fasten off.

Back

With WS of Band facing, skip 14 (19, 24, 29, 34) sts from right; attach yarn.

Row 1: Ch 4 (*counts as dc, ch-1, here and throughout*), skip 1 st, [dc in next, ch 1, skip 1] 12 times, dc in last, turn—27 sts.

Row 2: Ch 3 (*counts as 1st dc, here and throughout*), skip 1 st, dc in next 23 sts, skip 1 st, dc in last, turn—25 dc.

Row 3: Ch 4, skip 1 st, [dc in next, ch 1, skip 1] 11 times, dc in last, turn—25 sts.

Row 4: Ch 3, skip 1 st, dc in next 21 sts, skip 1 st, dc in last, turn—23 dc.

Row 5: Ch 4, skip 1 st, [dc in next, ch 1, skip 1] 10 times, dc in last, turn—23 sts.

Row 6: Ch 3, skip 1 st, dc in next 19 sts, skip 1 st, dc in last, turn—21 dc.

Row 7: Ch 4, skip 1 st, [dc in next ch 1, skip 1] 9 times, dc in last, turn—21 sts.

Row 8: Ch 3, skip 1 st, dc in next 17 sts, skip 1 st, dc in last, turn—19 dc.

Row 9: Ch 4, skip 1 st, [dc in next, ch 1, skip 1] 8 times, dc in last, turn—19 sts.

Row 10: Ch 3, skip 1 st, dc in next 15 sts, skip 1 st, dc in last, turn—17 dc.

Row 11: Ch 4, skip 1 st, [dc in next, ch 1, skip 1] 7 times, dc in last, turn—17 sts.

Row 12: Ch 3, skip 1 st, dc in next 13 sts, skip 1 st, dc in last, turn—15 dc.

Row 13: Ch 4, skip 1 st, [dc in next, ch 1, skip 1] 6 times, dc in last, turn—15 sts.

Row 14: Ch 3, skip 1 st, dc in next 11 sts, skip 1 st, dc in last—13 dc.

Fasten off.

Border

With WS of Band facing, join yarn in base of last st of Band Row 1.

Row 1: Ch 4 (*counts as dc, ch-1, here and throughout*), (dc, ch 1) in next 5 Band row ends, dc in last dc of Band Row 7, ch 20, dc in last st of Back Row 14, [ch 1, skip 1 st, dc in next] 5 times, ch 1, skip 1 st, dc in 1st st of Back Row 14, ch 20, dc in 1st st of Band Row 7, (dc, ch 1) in next 5 Band row ends, dc in base of 1st st of Band Row 1—23 dc, 2 ch-20 spaces.

Row 2: Ch 3 (*counts as 1st dc*), dc in each st across, turn—83 dc.

Row 3: Ch 4, skip 1 st, [dc in next, ch 1, skip 1 st] 40 times, dc in last—83 sts.

Fasten off and weave in ends.

Fringe

*Cut 20 in./51 cm strands of yarn. Fold in half evenly, at Border Row 3, with RS facing, work from left side of Band around to right, insert center fold of strand from RS to inside of Vest, pull ends through center loop and secure knot; repeat from * for each Border Row end, and between every 2 dc from Band Row 1. Trim fringe as desired.

Gray Skies Fingerless Mitts

Designed by Emily Truman

The texture of these gloves will keep you warm during the winter months but allow your fingers the freedom to text and tweet.

Skill Level
Intermediate

Sizes/Finished Measurements
Small (Medium, Large)
Palm Circumference: 8 (9, 10) in./20 (23, 25) cm
Length: 7 (7.5, 8) in./17.5 (19, 20) cm

Yarn

Cloudborn Superwash Highland Worsted, medium weight #4 yarn (100% Fine Highland superwash wool; 200 yd./183 m per 3.5 oz./100 g skein)
• 1 skein Graphite Heather

Hook & Other Materials
• US Size H-8 (5.0 mm) crochet hook
• Yarn needle

Gauge
16 sts and 11 rows in pattern st = 4 in./10 cm
Adjust hook size if necessary to obtain gauge.

Note
• Pattern is written for size Small with adjustments for larger sizes in parentheses.

Instructions (make 2)

Ch 31 (33, 35).

Row 1 (RS): Working in back bump for this row, dc in 4th ch from hook (*skipped chs count as 1st dc*) and in next 19 (21, 23), sc in next 8 chs, turn—29 (31, 33) sts here and throughout.

Row 2: Ch 1 (*not a st*), BLO sc in next 8, sl st in next, *dc in next, sl st in next; repeat from * across, turn.

Row 3: Ch 2 (*counts as 1st dc*), dc in next 20 (22, 24), BLO sc in next 8, turn.

Rows 4–24 (26, 26): Repeat Rows 2–3, ending on a repeat of Row 2.

Do not fasten off. Continue to Seaming.

Seaming

Fold piece in half, aligning Last Row with Row 1 and RS facing in. Ch 1, sl st through both loops and both layers for next 8, sl st through Last Row only for next 9 (*thumbhole made*), sl st through both loops and both layers for next 4 (6, 8), sl st through both loops of Row 1 and BLO of Last Row for last 8. Fasten off and weave in ends. Turn RS out.

Attach yarn with sc to top of Mitt at seam, *2 sc in next ch-2 space, 3 sc in next ch-2 space; repeat from * around, sl st to 1st sc to join.

Fasten off and weave in ends.

Thumb

With RS facing, join with sl st at bottom of thumbhole at seam.

Round 1: Ch 1, sc evenly around thumbhole, sl st to 1st sc to join.

Rounds 2–3: Ch 1, sc2tog, sc in each st to top of thumbhole, 2 sc in top of thumbhole, sc in each st on opposite side to last 2, sc2tog, sl st to 1st sc to join.

Fasten off and weave in ends.

Metallic Slippers

Designed by Salena Baca

These snug-fitting slippers are a perfect design if you're looking to work up your very first pair. Worked in simple rounds and repeats, you'll quickly make a pair with ease, all while having a lot of fun!

Skill Level
Easy

Sizes/Finished Measurements
US Women's Shoe Size: 5/6 (7/8, 9/10, 11/12)
Length: 9 (9.5, 10, 10.5) in./23 (24, 25, 27) cm

Yarn

Red Heart With Love Metallic, worsted weight #4 yarn (98% acrylic, 2% metallic; 200 yd./183 m per 4.5 oz./127 g skein)
- 1 skein Charcoal 8410 (Color A)
- 1 skein Black 8112 (Color B)

Hook & Other Materials
- US Size I-9 (5.5 mm) crochet hook
- Measuring tape
- Stitch marker
- Yarn needle

Gauge
14 sc and 14 rows = 4 in./10 cm

Notes
- Slippers are designed to be fitted; measure length of foot to determine size for best fit.
- Slippers are worked in three parts: Toe is worked in continuous rounds, Heel is formed in rows, and then Cuff is worked in rounds with contrasting color.
- A ch-1 at beginning of a row/round does not count as a st.
- Place stitch marker in last stitch of Round 1, and move as rounds are completed.
- Pattern is written for size 5/6 with adjustments for larger sizes in parentheses.

Instructions (make 2)

Toe

With Color A, ch 12 (13, 14, 15).

Round 1 (RS): Sc in 2nd ch from hook and each ch across, rotate to work in opposite side of starting ch, sc in each ch across, do not join—22 (24, 26, 28) sc.

Rounds 2–20 (22, 24, 26): Sc in each st around, do not join—22 (24, 26, 28) sc.

Do not fasten off. Continue to Heel.

Heel

Flatten toe. If not already at corner/side, sc to corner so Heel will be formed in line with Toe.

Rows 1–12: Ch 1, turn, sc in next 12 (14, 16, 18) sts—12 (14, 16, 18) sc.

Fasten off.

Cuff

Ensure RS is facing, join Color B into Right corner stitch of Heel at Row 12.

Round 1: Ch 1, sc in each st across Row 12, 2 sc in every even end row from left side of Heel, 1 sc in each st from Toe, 2 sc in every even end row from right side of Heel, sl st to 1st sc to join—46 (48, 50, 52) sc.

Round 2: Ch 1, sc2tog 12 (13, 14, 15) times, sc in next 10, sc2tog 6 times, sl st to 1st st to join—28 (29, 30, 31) sc.

Rounds 3–10: Ch 1, sc in each st around, sl st to 1st st to join—28 (29, 30, 31) sc.

Fasten off and weave in ends.

Sam Fingerless Mitts

Designed by Danyel Pink

These quick and colorful mitts are a delight to crochet. They are a must-have for texting, typing, gaming, and other activities that require your fingers to be free.

Skill Level
Intermediate

Finished Measurements
One size fits most teens/adults.
Width: 4.5 in./11.5 cm
Length: 6.25 in./16 cm

Yarn

Lion Brand Vanna's Choice Heathers, worsted weight #4 yarn (92% acrylic, 8% rayon; 145 yd./133 m per 3 oz./85 g skein)
- 1 skein Grey Marble 401 (Color A)

Lion Brand Vanna's Choice Solids, worsted weight #4 yarn (100% acrylic; 170 yd./156 m per 3.5 oz./100 g skein)
- 1 skein Eggplant 145 (Color B)
- 1 skein Peacock 176 (Color C)
- 1 skein Fern 171 (Color D)

Hooks & Other Materials
- US Size G-6 (4.0 mm) crochet hook
- US Size H-8 (5.0 mm) crochet hook
- Yarn needle

Gauge
7 sc and 8 rows = 2 in./5 cm
Adjust hook size if necessary to obtain gauge.

Special Stitch
Lsc (long single crochet) = Insert hook in indicated st 2 rows below, pull up loop to height of working row, yo and pull through both loops on hook.

Notes
- A ch-1 at the beginning of a row/round does not count as a st.

- To help hide seam, change colors at the ch-1 at the beginning of each round.
- Do not fasten off at each color change; carry unused yarn along inside of glove (see "Additional Resources" on page vii for link to video tutorial).

Instructions (make 2)

Cuff

With G-6 hook and Color A, ch 8.

Row 1: Sc in 2nd ch from hook and in each ch across—7 sc.

Rows 2–28: Ch 1, turn, sc in 1st st, sc in BL of next 5, sc in last st—7 sc.

Join end-to-end, ch 1, sl st first and last row together, forming the cuff. Do not fasten off. Turn cuff right-side-out.

Glove

Switch to H-8 hook and continue with Color A.

Round 1: Ch 1, sc in each end row of cuff, join to 1st sc—28 sc.

Round 2: Ch 1, [sc in next, ch 1, skip 1 st] around, join to 1st sc—14 sc, 14 ch-1 spaces.

Round 3: Switch to Color B. Ch 1, [sc in sc, Lsc in st below ch-1 space] around, join—14 sc, 14 Lsc.

Round 4: Switch to Color C. Ch 1, sc in each st around, join—28 sc.

Round 5: Switch to Color D. Ch 1, [sc in next, ch 1, skip 1 st] around, join—14 sc, 14 ch-1 spaces.

Round 6: Switch to Color A. Ch 1, [sc in sc, Lsc in st below ch-1 space] around, join—14 sc, 14 Lsc.

Round 7: Switch to Color B. Ch 1, sc in each st around, join—28 sc.

Round 8: Switch to Color C. Ch 1, [sc in next, ch 1, skip 1 st] around, join—14 sc, 14 ch-1 spaces.

Round 9: Switch to Color D. Ch 1, [sc in sc, Lsc in st below ch-1 space] around, join—14 sc, 14 Lsc.

Round 10: Switch to Color A. Ch 1, sc in each st around, join—28 sc.

Round 11: Switch to Color B. Ch 1, [sc in next, ch 1, skip 1 st] around, join—14 sc, 14 ch-1 spaces.

Round 12: Switch to Color C. Ch 1, [sc in sc, Lsc in st below ch-1 space] around, join—14 sc, 14 Lsc.

Round 13 (Left Glove Only): Switch to Color D. Ch 1, sc in next 2, ch 4 loosely, skip 4 sts (*thumbhole made*), sc in remaining 22 sts, join—24 sc, 1 ch-4 space.

Round 13 (Right Glove Only): Switch to Color D. Ch 1, sc in next 22, ch 4 loosely, skip 4 sts (*thumbhole made*), sc in remaining 2 sts, join—24 sc, 1 ch-4 space.

Round 14: Switch to Color A. Ch 1, [sc in next, ch 1, skip 1 st] around, join—14 sc, 14 ch-1 spaces.

Round 15: Switch to Color B. Ch 1, [sc in sc, Lsc in st below ch-1 space] around, join—14 sc, 14 Lsc. Fasten off Color B.

Round 16: Switch to Color C. Ch 1, sc in each st around, join—28 sc. Fasten off Color C.

Round 17: Switch to Color D. Ch 1, sc in each st around, join—28 sc. Fasten off Color D.

Round 18: Switch to Color A. Ch 1, sc in each st around, join—28 sc. Fasten off Color A.

Finishing

Weave in all ends.

Slightly Slipper Socks

Designed by Emily Truman

This sock is designed for that in-between time during fall and spring when slippers are too warm but you need a little something to cover your feet.

Skill Level
Intermediate

Sizes/Finished Measurements
Small (Medium, Large)
US Women's Shoe Sizes 6/7 (8/9, 10/11)
Length: 9 (9.5, 10) in./23 (24, 25) cm

Yarn

Hobby Lobby Yarn Bee Soft & Sleek Solids, medium weight #4 yarn (100% acrylic; 257 yd./235 m per 5 oz./142 g skein)
   • 1 skein Ivory 101 (Color A)
Hobby Lobby Yarn Bee Soft & Sleek Prints, medium weight #4 yarn (100% acrylic; 208 yd./190 m per 4 oz./113 g skein)
   • 1 skein Blushy 918 (Color B)

Hook & Other Materials
   • US Size I-9 (5.5 mm) crochet hook
   • Yarn needle

Gauge
7 hdc and 5 rows = 2 in./5 cm
Adjust hook size if necessary to obtain gauge.

Notes
   • Body is worked in joined rounds, sl st to 1st st of round to join. Heel is worked in rows.
   • Beginning ch-1 does not count as a st.
   • Pattern is written for size Small with adjustments for larger sizes in parentheses.

Instructions (make 2)

Toe (all sizes)

With Color A, ch 7.

Round 1: Hdc in 2nd ch from hook and in next 4 ch, 3 hdc in last ch, rotate to work on opposite side of beginning ch, hdc in next 4, 2 hdc in last, join—14 hdc.

Round 2: Ch 1, 2 hdc in same, hdc in next 4, 2 hdc in next 3, hdc in next 4, 2 hdc in next 2, join—20 hdc.

Round 3: Ch 1, 2 hdc in same, hdc in next 6, [2 hdc in next, hdc in next] twice, 2 hdc in next, hdc in next 5, 2 hdc in next, hdc in next, 2 hdc in next, join—26 hdc.

Round 4: Ch 1, hdc in each st around, join.

Round 5: Ch 1, 2 hdc in same, hdc in next 12, 2 hdc in next, hdc in next 12, join—28 hdc.

Fasten off Color A.

Body

Round 1: With Color B, ch 1, *2 hdc in next, skip 1; repeat from * around, join—28 hdc.

Round 2: With Color A, ch 1, sc in space before 1st hdc, ch 2, *skip 2 hdc, sc in space before next hdc, ch 2; repeat from * around, join—14 sc, 14 ch-2 spaces.

Round 3: With Color B, ch 1, 2 hdc in each ch-2 space around, join—28 hdc.

Rounds 4–14 (16, 18): Repeat Body Rounds 2–3, ending on a repeat of Round 2. Drop Color B for later use.

Heel

Worked in Rows. Turn before beginning.

Row 1 (WS): With Color A, ch 1, 3 sc in next 6 ch-2 spaces, turn—18 sc.

Row 2: Ch 1, sc2tog, sc in next 14, sc2tog, turn—16 sc.

Row 3: Ch 1, sc2tog, sc in next 12, sc2tog, turn—14 sc.

Row 4: Ch 1, sc2tog, sc in next 10, sc2tog, turn—12 sc.

Row 5: Ch 1, sc2tog, sc in next 8, sc2tog, turn—10 sc.

Row 6: Ch 1, sc2tog, sc in next 6, sc2tog, turn—8 sc.

Row 7: Ch 1, sc2tog, sc in next 4, sc2tog, turn—6 sc.

Row 8: Ch 1, sc2tog, sc in next 2, sc2tog, turn—4 sc.

Row 9: Ch 1, sc2tog twice, turn—2 sc.

Row 10: Ch 1, sc2tog, sc in side of next 2 rows, turn—3 sc.

Row 11: Ch 1, sc in next 3, sc in side of next 2 rows, turn—5 sc.

Row 12: Ch 1, sc in next 5, sc in side of next 2 rows, turn—7 sc.

Row 13: Ch 1, sc in next 7, sc in side of next 2 rows, turn—9 sc.

Row 14: Ch 1, sc in next 9, sc in side of next 2 rows, turn—11 sc.

Row 15: Ch 1, sc in next 11, sc in side of next 2 rows, turn—13 sc.

Row 16: Ch 1, sc in next 13, sc in side of next 2 rows, turn—15 sc.

Row 17: Ch 1, sc in next 15, sc in side of next 2 rows, turn—17 sc.

Row 18: Ch 1, sc in next 17, sc in side of next 2 rows, turn—19 sc.

Row 19: Ch 1, sc in next 19, sc in side of next row, sc2tog over side of next row and next st of Body, turn—21 sc.

Row 20: Ch 1, sc in next 21, sc in side of next row, sc2tog over side of next row and next st of Body, turn—23 sc.

Body (continued)

Round 15 (17, 19) (RS): Pick up Color B in next ch-2 space of Body, ch 1, 2 hdc in next 8 ch-2 spaces, working across Heel, *2 hdc in next, skip 1; repeat from * around, join—40 hdc.

Round 16 (18, 20): With Color A, ch 1, sc in space before 1st hdc, ch 1, *skip 2 hdc, sc in space before next hdc, ch 1; repeat from * around, join—20 sc, 20 ch-1 spaces.

Round 17 (19, 21): With Color B, ch 1, 2 hdc in each ch-1 space around, join—40 hdc.

Round 18 (20, 22): With Color A, repeat Round 16 (18, 20).

Round 19 (21, 23): With Color B, repeat Round 17 (19, 21). Fasten off Color B.

Cuff

Rounds 1–3 (RS): With Color A, ch 2 (*counts as BPhdc*), FPhdc around next, *BPhdc around next, FPhdc around next; repeat from * around, sl st to 2nd ch of beginning ch-2 to join—40 sts.

Pattern is written for ankle socks. Repeat last round as desired for more height.

Fasten off and weave in ends.

Sparkle Soft Cowl

*Designed by **Salena Baca***

The right yarn can make all the difference in making a stunning accessory! This simple pattern creates depth and texture, and the yarn offers a luxurious touch. Choose other yarn types and colors to fit your personality.

Skill Level
Easy

Sizes/Finished Measurements
Small (Medium, Large)
Circumference: 28 (30, 32) in./71 (76, 81) cm
Height: 13 (13, 13) in./33 (33, 33) cm

Yarn

Red Heart Gleam, medium weight #4 yarn (96% acrylic, 4% other fiber; 169 yd./154 m per 3.5 oz./100 g skein)
  • 2 skeins Patina 3520

Hook & Other Materials
  • US Size K-10 (6.5 mm) crochet hook
  • Yarn needle

Gauge
17 dc and 10 rows = 4 in./10 cm
Adjust hook size if necessary to obtain gauge.

Special Stitch
Cl (cluster) = [Yo and insert hook, yo and pull up loop, yo and pull through 2 loops on hook] 3 times in same st, yo and pull through remaining loops on hook.

Note
  • Pattern is written for size Small with adjustments for larger sizes in parentheses.

Instructions

Ch 130 (140, 150), taking care not to twist, sl st to 1st ch to form ring.

Round 1 (RS): Ch 2 (*not a st, now and throughout*), [Cl, ch 4, skip 4 sts, sc in next, ch 4, skip 4 sts] 13 (14, 15) times, sl st in top of 1st cluster to join—130 (140, 150) sts.

Round 2: Ch 1, [sc in next Cl, ch 4, bobble in next sc, ch 4] 13 (14, 15) times, sl st to 1st sc to join—130 (140, 150) sts.

Rounds 3–20: Repeat Rounds 1–2.

Round 21: Ch 1 (*not a st*), 3 sc in each ch-4 space around, sl st to 1st sc to join—78 (84, 90) sc. Fasten off.

Finishing

With RS facing, join yarn to 1st ch-4 space of Round 1, ch 1, 3 sc in each ch-4 space around, sl st to 1st sc to join. Fasten off and weave in ends.

Sprightly Boot Cuffs

Designed by Salena Baca

Boot cuffs are a great way to top your boots, keep the cold out, and layer an outfit! This pair is just long enough to let the stitching detail peek out over the edge of your boots.

Skill Level
Intermediate

Sizes/Finished Measurements
Small (Medium, Large, XL)
Circumference: 12 (13, 14, 15) in./30.5 (33, 35.5, 38) cm
Height: 7.5 in./19 cm (all sizes)

Yarn

Sprightly Acrylic Wool Worsted, worsted weight #4 yarn (80% acrylic, 20% wool; 216 yd./198 m per 3.5 oz./100 g skein)
• 1 skein Copper

Hook & Other Materials
• US Size J-10 (6.0 mm) crochet hook

Gauge
14.25 sts and 11 rows = 4 in./10 cm
Adjust hook size if necessary to obtain gauge.

Special Stitches
rt post st (right post stitch) = Yo, insert hook in sc, yo and pull up a loop, yo and pull through 2 loops, yo twice, skip next sc, insert hook around next dc 2 rows below, yo and pull up a loop, [yo and pull through 2 loops] twice, yo and pull through all 3 loops on hook.
lf post st (left post stitch) = Yo twice, insert hook around same st as rt post st 2 rows below, yo and pull up a loop, [yo and pull through 2 loops] twice, yo, insert hook in sc, yo and pull up a loop, yo and pull through 2 loops, yo and pull through all 3 loops on hook.

Notes
• For best fit, measure around calf where cuff will be worn. Follow smallest size instructions that are closest to this measurement.

- Pattern is written for size Small with adjustments for larger sizes in parentheses.
- Pattern is written in two sections: the Cuff is worked in rows, and then the Body is worked in rounds.
- Beginning ch-1 and ch-2 do not count as a st.

Instructions (make 2)

Cuff

Ch 11.

Row 1: Sc in 2nd ch from hook and in each ch across, turn—10 sc.

Row 2: Ch 1, sc in BLO of each st across, turn—10 sc.

Rows 3–42 (46, 50, 54): Repeat Row 2. Do not fasten off.

Hold Row 1 together with Row 42 (46, 50, 54), sl st together to join, turn cuff inside out so that seam is on the inside.

Body

With RS of Cuff facing, Ch 1.

Round 1 (RS): 2 sc in every other sc end row from Cuff, sl st to top of 1st sc to join—42 (46, 50, 54) sc.

Round 2: Ch 2, dc in each st around, sl st to top of 1st dc to join—42 (46, 50, 54) dc.

Round 3: Ch 1, sc in each st around, sl st to top of 1st sc to join—42 (46, 50, 54) sc.

Round 4: Ch 2, dc in next 15 sts, ch 1, skip 1 st, [rt post st in next sc, dc in next 3 sts, lf post st in next sc, ch 1, skip 1 st] 2 times, dc in last 14 (18, 22, 26) sts, sl st to top of 1st dc to join—42 (46, 50, 54) sts.

Round 5: Ch 1, sc in next 15 sts, ch 1, skip 1 st, [sc in next 5 sts, ch 1, skip 1 st] 2 times, sc in last 14 (18, 22, 26) sts, sl st to top of 1st sc to join—42 (46, 50, 54) sc.

Rounds 6–10: Repeat Rounds 4 and 5, ending on a repeat of Round 4.

Rounds 11–13: Ch 1, sc in each st around, sl st to top of 1st st to join—42 (46, 50, 54) sc.

Fasten off and weave in ends.

Sunburst Scarf

Designed by Danyel Pink

The beautiful ombre yarn and openwork detailing are sure to make this your new favorite scarf! It will certainly keep you warm and cozy this winter.

Skill Level
Intermediate

Finished Measurements
Width: 6.5 in./16.5 cm
Length (excluding fringe): 65 in./165 cm

Yarn

Lion Brand Scarfie, bulky weight #5 yarn (78% acrylic, 22% wool; 312 yd./285 m per 5.4 oz./153 g skein)
• 1 skein Mint/Silver 217

Hook & Other Materials
• US Size K-10.5 (6.5 mm) crochet hook
• Yarn needle

Gauge
6 dc and 3 rows = 2 in./5 cm
Gauge is not critical to this project.

Notes
• Beginning ch-3 of each row counts as a dc.
• The 2 double crochets worked together at the beginning/end of each odd-numbered row count as a dc-group.
• Work ch-4 and ch-5 spaces in the sunburst sections snugly, or the center of the design will lack proper definition.

Instructions

Ch 21.

Row 1: Dc in 4th ch from hook, skip 1 ch, 3 dc in next, [skip 2 chs, 3 dc in next] 4 times, skip 1 ch, dc in last 2 chs—19 dc.

Row 2: Ch 3, turn, [3 dc in space between dc-groups] 3 times, ch 10, [3 dc in space between dc-groups] 3 times, dc in top of turning ch—20 dc, 1 ch-10 space.

Row 3: Ch 3, turn, dc in same st, [3 dc in space between dc-groups] twice, ch 4, sc in ch-10 space, ch 4, [3 dc in space between dc-groups] twice, 2 dc in top of turning ch—16 dc, 2 ch-4 spaces, 1 sc.

Row 4: Ch 3, turn, [3 dc in space between dc-groups] twice, ch 4, sc in ch-4 space, sc in sc, sc in ch-4 space, ch 4, [3 dc in space between dc-groups] twice, dc in top of turning ch—14 dc, 2 ch-4 spaces, 3 sc.

Row 5: Ch 3, turn, dc in same st, 3 dc in space between dc-groups, ch 4, sc in ch-4 space, sc in next 3 sc, sc in ch-4 space, ch 4, 3 dc in space between dc-groups, 2 dc in top of turning ch—10 dc, 2 ch-4 spaces, 5 sc.

Row 6: Ch 3, turn, 3 dc in space between dc-groups, ch 4, sc in ch-4 space, sc in next 5 sc, sc in ch-4 space, ch 4, 3 dc in space between dc-groups, dc in top of turning ch—8 dc, 2 ch-4 spaces, 7 sc.

Row 7: Ch 3, turn, dc in same st, ch 4, sc in ch-4 space, sc in next 7 sc, sc in ch-4 space, ch 4, 2 dc in top of turning ch—4 dc, 2 ch-4 spaces, 9 sc.

Row 8: Ch 3, turn, 3 dc in ch-4 space, ch 4, skip 1 sc, sc in next 7 sc, skip 1 sc, ch 4, 3 dc in ch-4 space, dc in top of turning ch—8 dc, 2 ch-4 spaces, 7 sc.

Row 9: Ch 3, turn, dc in same st, 3 dc in ch-4 space, ch 4, skip 1 sc, sc in next 5 sc, skip 1 sc, ch 4, 3 dc in ch-4 space, 2 dc in top of turning ch—10 dc, 2 ch-4 spaces, 5 sc.

Row 10: Ch 3, turn, 3 dc in space between dc-groups, 3 dc in ch-4 space, ch 4, skip 1 sc, sc in next 3 sc, skip 1 sc, ch 4, 3 dc in ch-4 space, 3 dc in space between dc-groups, dc in top of turning ch—14 dc, 2 ch-4 spaces, 3 sc.

Row 11: Ch 3, turn, dc in same st, 3 dc in space between dc-groups, 3 dc in ch-4 space, ch 5, skip 1 sc, sc in next sc, skip 1 sc, ch 5, 3 dc in ch-4 space, 3 dc in space between dc-groups, 2 dc in top of turning ch—16 dc, 2 ch-5 spaces, 1 sc.

Row 12: Ch 3, turn, [3 dc in space between dc-groups] twice, [3 dc in ch-5 space] twice, [3 dc in space between dc-groups] twice, dc in top of turning ch—20 dc.

Row 13: Ch 3, turn, dc in same st, [3 dc in space between dc-groups] 5 times, 2 dc in top of turning ch—19 dc.

Row 14: Ch 3, turn, [3 dc in space between dc-groups] 6 times, dc in top of turning ch—20 dc.

Row 15: Repeat Row 13.

Rows 16–111: Repeat Rows 2–15 seven times, ending last repeat on Row 13.

Note: For shorter/longer scarf, complete the repeat above to desired length.

Fringe

*Cut forty 12 in./30.5 cm lengths of yarn, fold one strand in half, insert loop into 1st st along end of scarf, pull ends of fringe through loop, and pull to secure; repeat from * for all sts on both ends of scarf.

Trim fringe if desired.

Finishing

Fasten off and weave in ends.

Block scarf to straighten edges and enhance sunburst sections if desired.

Bags & Totes

Bloom Market Tote

Designed by Salena Baca

This one-piece, bottom-up market tote is designed just like a classic granny square. Changing the color for the last few rounds will give your project a pop, turning this classic design into a timeless tote.

Skill Level
Intermediate

Finished Measurements
Circumference: 30 in./76 cm
Height: 11 in./28 cm

Yarn
Scheepjes Bloom, worsted weight #4 yarn (100% cotton; 87 yd./80 m per 1.76 oz./50 g skein)
- 2 skeins Grey Thistle 421 (Color A)
- 1 skein Forget-Me-Not 419 (Color B)

Hook & Other Materials
- US Size H-8 (5.0 mm) crochet hook
- Measuring tape

Gauge
5 pattern rows and 16 sts = 4 in./10 cm

Notes
- Beginning ch-1 does not count as a st.
- Beginning ch-3 counts as 1st dc.

Instructions

With Color A, make magic ring (see "Additional Resources" on page vii for link to video tutorial).

Round 1 (RS): Ch 3, 3 dc in ring, ch 3, [4 dc in ring, ch 3] 3 times, join—16 dc, 4 ch-3 spaces.

Round 2: Sl st to 1st ch-3 space, ch 3, (3 dc, ch 3, 4 dc) in same ch-3 space, ch 3, (4 dc, ch 3, 4 dc, ch 3) in each ch-3 space around, join—32 dc, 8 ch-3 spaces.

Round 3: Sl st to 1st corner ch-3 space, ch 3, (3 dc, ch 3, 4 dc) in same space, (ch 3, dc, ch 3) in next ch-3 space, [(4 dc, ch 3, 4 dc) in corner ch-3 space, (ch 3, dc, ch 3) in next ch-3 space] 3 times, join—36 dc, 12 ch-3 spaces.

Round 4: Sl st to 1st corner ch-3 space, ch 3, (3 dc, ch 3, 4 dc) in same space, ch 3, (dc, ch 3) in next 2 ch-3 spaces, [(4 dc, ch 3, 4 dc) in corner ch-3 space,

ch 3 (dc, ch 3) in each side ch-3 space] 3 times, join—40 dc, 16 ch-3 spaces.

Round 5: Sl st to 1st corner ch-3 space, ch 3, (3 dc, ch 3, 4 dc) in same space, ch 3, (dc, ch 3) in next 3 ch-3 spaces, [(4 dc, ch 3, 4 dc) in corner ch-3 space, ch 3, (dc, ch 3) in each side ch-3 space] 3 times, join—44 dc, 20 ch-3 spaces.

Round 6: Sl st to 1st corner ch-3 space, ch 3, (3 dc, ch 3, 4 dc) in same space, ch 3, (dc, ch 3) in next 4 ch-3 spaces, [(4 dc, ch 3, 4 dc) in corner ch-3 space, ch 3, (dc, ch 3) in each side ch-3 space] 3 times, join—48 dc, 24 ch-3 spaces.

Round 7: Sl st to 1st corner ch-3 space, ch 3, (3 dc, ch 3, 4 dc) in same space, ch 3, (dc, ch 3) in next 5 ch-3 spaces, [(4 dc, ch 3, 4 dc) in corner ch-3 space, ch 3, (dc, ch 3) in each side ch-3 space] 3 times, join—52 dc, 28 ch-3 spaces.

Round 8: Sl st to 1st corner ch-3 space, ch 3, (3 dc, ch 3, 4 dc) in same space, ch 3, (dc, ch 3) in next 6 ch-3 spaces, [(4 dc, ch 3, 4 dc) in corner ch-3 space, ch 3, (dc, ch 3) in each side ch-3 space] 3 times, join—56 dc, 32 ch-3 spaces.

Round 9: Sl st to 1st corner ch-3 space, ch 3, (3 dc, ch 3, 4 dc) in same space, ch 3, (dc, ch 3) in next 7 ch-3 spaces, [(4 dc, ch 3, 4 dc) in corner ch-3 space, ch 3, (dc, ch 3) in each side ch-3 space] 3 times, join—60 dc, 36 ch-3 spaces.

Round 10: Sl st to 1st corner ch-3 space, ch 3, (3 dc, ch 3, 4 dc) in same space, ch 3, (dc, ch 3) in next 8 ch-3 spaces, [(4 dc, ch 3, 4 dc) in corner ch-3 space, ch 3, (dc, ch 3) in each side ch-3 space] 3 times, join—64 dc, 40 ch-3 spaces.

Round 11: Sl st to 1st corner ch-3 space, ch 3, (3 dc, ch 3, 4 dc) in same space, ch 3, (dc, ch 3) in next 9 ch-3 spaces, [(4 dc, ch 3, 4 dc) in corner ch-3 space, ch 3, (dc, ch 3) in each side ch-3 space] 3 times, join—68 dc, 44 ch-3 spaces.

Round 12: Sl st to 1st corner ch-3 space, ch 3, (3 dc, ch 3, 4 dc) in same space, ch 3, (dc, ch 3) in next 10 ch-3 spaces, [(4 dc, ch 3, 4 dc) in corner ch-3 space, ch 3, (dc, ch 3) in each side ch-3 space] 3 times, join—72 dc, 48 ch-3 spaces.

Round 13: Sl st to 1st corner ch-3 space, ch 3, (3 dc, ch 3, 4 dc) in same space, ch 3, (dc, ch 3) in next 11 ch-3 spaces, [(4 dc, ch 3, 4 dc) in corner ch-3 space, ch 3, (dc, ch 3) in each side ch-3 space] 3 times, join—76 dc, 52 ch-3 spaces.

Round 14: Sl st to 1st corner ch-3 space, ch 3, (3 dc, ch 3, 4 dc) in same space, ch 3, (dc, ch 3) in next 12 ch-3 spaces, [(4 dc, ch 3, 4 dc) in corner ch-3 space, ch 3, (dc, ch 3) in each side ch-3 space] 3 times, join—80 dc, 56 ch-3 spaces.

Round 15: Sl st to 1st corner ch-3 space, ch 3, (3 dc, ch 3, 4 dc) in same space, ch 3, (dc, ch 3) in next 13 ch-3 spaces, [(4 dc, ch 3, 4 dc) in corner ch-3 space, ch 3, (dc, ch 3) in each side ch-3 space] 3 times, join—84 dc, 60 ch-3 spaces.

Round 16: Sl st to 1st corner ch-3 space, ch 3, (3 dc, ch 3, 4 dc) in same space, dc in next 14 ch-3 spaces, [(4 dc, ch 3, 4 dc) in corner ch-3 space, dc in each side ch-3 space] 3 times, join, fasten off color A—88 dc, 4 ch-3 spaces.

Round 17: With Color B, ch 1, sc in same, sc in each st until 2nd ch from ch-3 space met, *ch 40 (*tote handle*), sc in 2nd ch from next ch-3 space, sc in each st until 2nd ch from next ch-3 space met; repeat from * one more time, sc in each st around, join—132 sts.

Rounds 18–19: Ch 1, sc in each st around, join—132 sc.

Round 20: Sl st loosely in each st around, join, fasten off—132 sl sts.

Finishing

Attach Color B in any dc from Round 16, sl st loosely in each st around top of Round 16 and bottom of Round 17 (*reinforces handle*). Fasten off. Repeat for opposite handle.

Weave in all ends.

Concert Clutch

Designed by Emily Truman

Many stadiums and other venues are limiting purse sizes to 6.5 x 4.5 in./16.5 x 11.5 cm for security. The small size fits within those dimensions, but the bigger sizes are available when you need a little more space.

Skill Level
Intermediate

Sizes/Finished Measurements
Small (Medium, Large)
Width: 6 (8, 10) in./15 (20, 25) cm
Height: 4.5 (5.5, 6.5) in./11.5 (14, 16.5) cm

Yarn

Red Heart Strata, bulky #5 weight (76% acrylic, 24% nylon; 95 yd./86 m per 3.5 oz./100 g skein)
- 1 (1, 2) skeins Navy 2860

Hook & Other Materials
- US Size 7.0 mm crochet hook
- Yarn needle
- 6 (8, 10) in./15 (20, 25) cm zipper
- Matching thread and sewing needle
- 0.5 in./1.25 cm swivel snap hook

Gauge
6 hdc and 4 rows = 2 in./5 cm
Adjust hook size if necessary to obtain gauge.

Note
- Pattern is written for size Small with adjustments for larger sizes in parentheses.

Instructions

Ch 17 (21, 25).

Round 1 (RS): Hdc in 2nd ch from hook and in each ch across, 4 hdc in last, rotate to work in opposite side of beginning ch, hdc in next 14 (18, 22), 3 hdc in same st as 1st hdc, sl st to 1st st to join—36 (44, 52) sts here and throughout.

Round 2: Ch 1 (*not a st here and throughout*), *FPdc around next, hdc in next 3; repeat from * around, sl st to 1st st to join.

Round 3: Ch 1, hdc in 1st, *FPdc around next, hdc in next 3; repeat from * around to last 3, FPdc around next, hdc in next 2, sl st to 1st st to join.

Round 4: Ch 1, hdc in 1st 2, *FPdc around next, hdc in next 3; repeat from * around to last 2, FPdc around next, hdc in next, sl st to 1st st to join.

Round 5: Ch 1, *hdc in next 3, FPdc around next; repeat from * around, sl st to 1st st to join.

Rounds 6–9 (11, 13): Repeat Rounds 2–5, ending on a repeat of Round 5 (3, 5).

Continue to Handle.

Handle

Ch 30, sl st through swivel side of swivel snap hook and in each ch back to last round. Fasten off and weave in ends.

Zipper

With sewing needle and matching thread, sew zipper to attach to Clutch. Snap swivel snap hook to zipper pull. With zipper closed, zipper pull should be on same side as Handle and swivel snap hook.

Curio Coin Purse

Designed by Emily Truman

Vintage coin purses are classy, fun, and functional. This one is made with cotton thread for a very fine texture.

Skill Level
Intermediate

Finished Measurements
Width: 5 in./12.5 cm
Height (not including clasp): 4.5 in./11.5 cm

Yarn
Knit Picks Curio #10 Crochet Thread (100% cotton; 721 yd./670 m per 3.5 oz./100 g skein)
• 1 skein Ciel 26268

Hook & Other Materials
• US Size B-1 (2.25 mm) crochet hook
• Stitch marker
• Yarn needle
• 3.75 in. x 2 in./9.5 x 5 cm coin purse clasp
• Sewing needle to fit through holes in clasp

Gauge
[Sc, dc] 8 times and 16 rows = 2 in./5 cm
Adjust hook size if necessary to obtain gauge.

Notes
• Beginning ch-1 does not count as a st. To join, sl st to 1st st of round.
• Directions are given to adjust sewing on clasp, due to differences in clasp sizes and availability.

Instructions

Ch 21.

Round 1 (RS): Sc in 2nd ch from hook and in next 18, 3 sc in last ch, rotate to work on opposite side of ch, sc in next 18, 2 sc in last, join—42 sc.

Round 2: Ch 1, 2 sc in 1st, sc in next 18, 2 sc in next 3, sc in next 18, 2 sc in last 2, join—48 sc.

Round 3: Ch 1, 2 sc in 1st, sc in next, sc in next 18, [2 sc in next, sc in next] 3 times, sc in next 18, [2 sc in next, sc in next] 2 times, join—54 sc.

Round 4: Ch 1, 2 sc in 1st, sc in next 2, sc in next 18, [2 sc in next, sc in next 2] 3 times, sc in next 18, [2 sc in next, sc in next 2] 2 times, join—60 sc.

Round 5: Ch 1, 2 sc in 1st, sc in next 3, sc in next 18, [2 sc in next, sc in next 3] 3 times, sc in next 18, [2 sc in next, sc in next 3] 2 times, join—66 sc.

Round 6: Ch 1, 2 sc in 1st, sc in next 4, sc in next 18, [2 sc in next, sc in next 4] 3 times, sc in next 18, [2 sc in next, sc in next 4] 2 times, join—72 sc.

Round 7: Ch 1, 2 sc in 1st, sc in next 5, sc in next 18, [2 sc in next, sc in next 5] 3 times, sc in next 18, [2 sc in next, sc in next 5] 2 times, join—78 sc.

*For smaller clasp sizes, skip to Round 9.

Round 8: Ch 1, 2 sc in 1st, sc in next 6, sc in next 18, [2 sc in next, sc in next 6] 3 times, sc in next 18, [2 sc in next, sc in next 6] 2 times, join—84 sc.

Round 9 (RS): Ch 1, *(sc, dc) in next, skip 1; repeat from * around, join, turn—84 sts.

Rounds 10–34: Ch 1, *(sc, dc) in next sc; repeat from * around, join, turn—84 sts.

Fasten off, leaving a long tail to attach clasp.

Attach Clasp

Due to clasp differences, count the holes on one side of clasp. Divide that number into 84 (total sts in last round), rounding if needed. That answer will be the number of sts to pick up on Round 34 with each needle insertion. For example, a clasp with 30 holes on one side does not divide into 84 evenly, but does divide into 90; 90 divided by 30 equals 3, so with each needle insertion, weave needle in and out of 3 sts on Round 34 before bringing the needle back out of clasp. Due to rounding approximations for this example, pick up only 2 sts on 6 needle insertions to even out. Most clasps will need between 2–5 sts picked up with each needle insertion. Sew clasp to purse in this manner.

Fasten off and weave in ends.

Fine Wine Tote

Designed by Danyel Pink

Wine totes make fabulous host/hostess gifts! This tote has a great texture and fits most wine, champagne, or sparkling juice bottles.

Skill Level
Easy

Finished Measurements
Fits most 750 ml bottles.
Circumference: 13 in./33 cm
Height: 11.5 in./29 cm

Yarn

Bernat Handicrafter, worsted weight #4 yarn (100% cotton; 80 yd./73 m per 1.75 oz./50 g skein)
 • 2 skeins Soft Violet 97

Hook & Other Materials
 • US Size H-8 (5.0 mm) crochet hook
 • Yarn needle

Gauge
7 dc and 4 rows = 2 in./5 cm
Adjust hook size if necessary to obtain gauge.

Special Stitch
Puff (puff stitch) = [Yo and insert hook in designated space, yo and pull up loop] 3 times, yo and pull through all 7 loops on hook.

Note
 • A ch-1 at the beginning of a round does not count as a st.

Instructions

Ch 4, sl st to 1st ch to form ring.

Round 1: Ch 1, 11 hdc in ring, sl st to 1st st—11 hdc.

Round 2: Ch 1, 2 hdc in each st around, sl st to 1st st—22 hdc.

Round 3: Ch 1, hdc in 1st st, 2 hdc in next, [hdc in next, 2 hdc in next] around, sl st to 1st st—33 hdc.

Round 4: Ch 1, hdc in 1st 2 sts, 2 hdc in next, [hdc in next 2, 2 hdc in next] around, sl st to 1st st—44 hdc.

Note: Circle should measure 3.75 in./9.5 cm diameter.

Round 5: Ch 4 (*counts as dc, ch-1 now and throughout*), skip next st, [dc in next, ch 1, skip 1 st] around, sl st to 3rd ch of beginning ch-4—22 dc, 22 ch-1 spaces.

Round 6: Sl st in ch-1 space, ch 1, Puff in same space, ch 1, [Puff in next st, ch 1] around, sl st to 1st st—22 Puffs, 22 ch-1 spaces.

Round 7: Ch 4, [dc in next ch-1 space, ch 1] around, sl st to 3rd ch of beginning ch-4—22 dc, 22 ch-1 spaces.

Rounds 8–26: Repeat Rows 6–7 nine times, and then repeat Row 6 once more.

Round 27: Ch 1, 2 sc in each ch-1 space around, sl st to 1st st—44 sc.

Round 28: Ch 1, sc in 1st 7 sts, ch 12, skip 8 sts, sc in next 14, ch 12, skip 8 sts, sc in next 7, sl st to 1st st—28 sc, 2 ch-12 spaces.

Round 29: Ch 1, sc in 1st 5 sts, sc2tog, sc in next 12 ch, sc2tog, sc in next 10, sc2tog, sc in next 12 ch, sc2tog, sc in next 5, sl st to 1st st—48 sts.

Round 30: Ch 1, sc in 1st 4 sts, sc2tog, sc in next 12, sc2tog, sc in next 8, sc2tog, sc in next 12, sc2tog, sc in next 4, sl st to 1st st—44 sts.

Round 31: Ch 1, sc in 1st 3 sts, sc2tog, sc in next 12, sc2tog, sc in next 6, sc2tog, sc in next 12, sc2tog, sc in next 3, sl st to 1st st—40 sts.

Finishing

Fasten off and weave in all ends.

Mandala Handbag

Designed by Emily Truman

Color-changing yarn and cables combine to produce
a one-of-a-kind result!

Skill Level
Intermediate

Finished Measurements
Width: 12 in./30.5 cm
Height: 11 in./28 cm

Yarn

Lion Brand Mandala, light weight #3 yarn (100% acrylic; 590 yd./540 m per
5.3 oz./150 g skein)
• 1 skein Chimera 204

Hook & Other Materials
• US Size G-6 (4.0 mm) crochet hook
• Purse handle
• Yarn needle
• Sewing thread and needle (optional)

Gauge
16 hdc and 14 rows = 4 in./10 cm
Adjust hook size if necessary to obtain gauge.

Special Stitch
FPdc cluster (front post double crochet cluster) = [Yo and insert hook
around post of st indicated from front to back to front, yo and pull up
a loop, yo and pull through 2 loops] 3 times, yo and pull through all 4
loops on hook.

Note
• Body is worked in joined rounds, slip stitch to 1st st of round to join.

Instructions

Ch 53.

Round 1: 3 hdc in 2nd ch from hook, hdc in each st across to last, 3 hdc in last, rotate, hdc in each st across opposite side of beginning ch, join—106 hdc.

Round 2: Ch 1 (*not a st now and throughout*), [2 hdc in next 3, hdc in next 50] twice, join—112 hdc.

Round 3: Ch 1, *skip 1, FPdc cluster around next, hdc in same and in next 6; repeat from * around working last hdc in sl st from previous round, join—14 clusters, 98 hdc.

Round 4: Ch 1, hdc in same and in each st around, join—112 hdc.

Round 5: Ch 1, skip same and next, *FPdc cluster around post of next st 2 rounds below (*just to the left of cluster*), hdc in top of same st and in next 6, skip 1; repeat from * around working last hdc in sl st from previous round, join—14 clusters, 98 hdc.

Rounds 6–37: Repeat Rounds 4–5.

Round 38: Ch 1, sc in each st around, join—112 sc. Fasten off and weave in ends.

Finishing

Attach purse handles in between cables with yarn needle and yarn, or with needle and sewing thread, following manufacturer's instructions.

Twisted Phone or Tablet Cozy

Designed by Emily Truman

Keep all your devices safe and cozy with some bright cotton yarn and a tight stitch pattern.

Skill Level
Intermediate

Sizes/Finished Measurements
Standard Phone (Plus-size Phone, Mini Tablet, Standard Tablet)
Width: 3 (3.5, 6, 7.5) in./7.5 (9, 15, 19) cm
Height: 6 (6.5, 9, 10) in./15 (16.5, 23, 25) cm

Yarn
Lion Brand 24/7 Cotton, worsted weight #4 yarn (100% cotton;
  186 yd./170 m per 3.5 oz./100 g skein)
  • 1 skein Jade 178 (Color A)
  • 1 skein Lilac 143 (Color B)
  • 1 skein Silver 149 (Color C)

Hook & Other Materials
  • US Size I-9 (5.5 mm) crochet hook
  • 1 button (1 in./2.5 cm)
  • Yarn needle

Gauge
[Sc3tog, ch-1] 4 times and 8 rows = 2.5 in./6.5 cm
Adjust hook size if necessary to obtain gauge.

Special Stitch
sc3tog (single crochet 3 stitches together) = [Insert hook in next st, yo and
  pull up a loop] 3 times, yo and pull through all loops on hook.

Notes
  • Cozy is worked from the bottom up in joined/turned rounds. When
    working in this manner, the 1st st of the new round will be the sl st
    from the previous round. Always skip that sl st, and begin round in
    next st.
  • Beginning ch-1 does not count as a st. When instructed to join, sl st to
    1st st of round.
  • Keep a loose tension throughout.

- Do not fasten off at each color change; carry unused yarn to WS of Cozy (see "Additional Resources" on page vii for link to video tutorial).
- To adjust size for your device, make a beginning ch as long as one side of device and continue with pattern.
- Pattern is written for Standard Phone size with adjustments for larger sizes in parentheses.

Instructions

With Color A, ch 12 (14, 24, 28).

Round 1 (RS): Sc in 2nd ch from hook and in each ch across, 2 sc in last ch, rotate to work on opposite side of ch, sc in each ch across, join, turn—22 (26, 46, 54) sc.

Round 2: With Color B, ch 1, sc3tog over next 3 sts, ch 1, *sc3tog beginning in last leg of previous st and over next 2 sts, ch 1; repeat from * around, last leg of last st will be completed in 1st st of round, ch 1, join, turn—22 (26, 46, 54) sts.

Rounds 3–16 (19, 24, 27): Repeat Round 2, alternating Color A, B, and C each round.
Fasten off Color B and Color C.

Buttonhole

Round 1 (RS): With Color A, ch 1, sc in each st and ch around, join—22 (26, 46, 54) sc.

Round 2: Ch 1, sc in each st to middle of Cozy, ch 11 (*buttonhole formed*), sc in each remaining st, join—22 (26, 46, 54) sc, 1 ch-11 space.

Round 3: Sl st in each sc and ch around.
Weave in all ends.

Finishing

Fasten off and weave in ends. Attach button on Cozy opposite buttonhole.

Kitchen &

Dining

Blackberry Coffee Cozy

Designed by Danyel Pink

Protect your hands from hot coffee, or soak up condensation from an icy cold soda. The texture on this cozy offers an extra bit of grip, too!

Skill Level
Intermediate

Finished Measurements
Fits most to-go cups or pint glasses.
Circumference: 9.5 in./24 cm
Height: 3.25 in./8 cm

Yarn

Lion Brand Kitchen Cotton, worsted weight #4 yarn (100% cotton; 99 yd./90 m per 2 oz./56.5 g skein)
• 1 skein Snap Pea 130 (Color A)
• 1 skein Grape 147 (Color B)

Hook & Other Materials
• US Size G-6 (4.0 mm) crochet hook
• Yarn needle

Gauge
14 sc = 4 in./10 cm; stitch height not critical.
Adjust hook size if necessary to obtain gauge.

Special Stitch
BB (blackberry stitch) = Draw up loop in next sc, [yo, draw through last loop on hook] 3 times, keeping ch-3 just made to RS of work, yo and draw through both loops on hook.

Notes
• The ch-1 at the beginning of a round does not count as a st.
• Do not fasten off when changing colors; hold unused color loosely along inside of work.
• Cozy may seem snug at first. Use caution if placing on a hot cup. Warmth and/or moisture will allow Cozy to expand slightly and fit perfectly.

Instructions

With Color A, ch 34, sl st in 1st ch to form circle.

Round 1 (RS): Ch 1, sc in each ch around, with Color B sl st to 1st sc to join—34 sc.

Round 2: Ch 1, *sc in BL of next st, BB in next st; repeat from * around, with Color A sl st to 1st sc to join—17 sc, 17 BB.

Round 3: Ch 1, *sc in FL of sc 2 rows below, sc in BB; repeat from * around, sl st to 1st sc to join—34 sc.

Round 4: Ch 1, sc in each sc around, with Color B sl st to 1st sc to join—34 sc.

Round 5: Ch 1, *BB in next st; sc in BL of next st; repeat from * around, with Color A sl st to 1st sc to join—17 sc, 17 BB.

Round 6: Ch 1, *sc in BB, sc in FL of sc 2 rows below; repeat from * around, sl st to 1st sc to join—34 sc.

Round 7: Ch 1, sc in each sc around, with Color B sl st to 1st sc to join—34 sc.

Rounds 8–10: Repeat Round 2–4.

Round 11: Ch 1, hdc in each sc around, sl st to 1st hdc to join—34 hdc.

Rounds 12–14: Repeat Round 11.

Fasten off and weave in all ends.

Hanging Herb Holder

Designed by Salena Baca

This quick and easy holder will hang all your favorite herbs, flowers, vines, and succulents! This piece is great for indoor or outdoor use, and makes a lovely gift item, too.

Skill Level
Easy

Finished Measurements
Base (diameter): 7 in./17.5 cm
Length (full hanging height): 23 in./58 cm

Yarn

Bernat Handicrafter, worsted weight #4 yarn (100% cotton; 80 yd./73 m per 1.75 oz./50 g skein)
• 1 skein Hot Green 13712

Hook & Other Materials
• US Size H-8 (5.0 mm) crochet hook
• Measuring tape
• Flower pot (4–7 in./10–17.5 cm high x 4–7 in./10–17.5 cm wide)
• 2 in./5 cm hook screw (to hang)

Gauge
17 dc = 4 in./10 cm and 5 dc rows = 3.5 in./9 cm
Adjust hook size if necessary to obtain gauge.

Instructions

Make magic ring (see "Additional Resources" on page vii for link to video tutorial).

Round 1 (RS): Ch 3 (*counts as 1st dc, now and throughout*), 11 dc in ring, sl st to join—12 dc.

Round 2: Ch 3, dc in same st, 2 dc in each st around, sl st to join—24 dc.

Round 3: Ch 3, dc in same st, dc in next, *2 dc in next, dc in next; repeat from * around, sl st to join—36 dc.

Round 4: Ch 3, dc in same st, dc in next 2, *2 dc in next, dc in next 2; repeat from * around, sl st to join—48 dc.

Round 5: Ch 3, dc in same st, dc in next 3, *2 dc in next, dc in next 3; repeat from * around, sl st to join—60 dc.

Round 6: Ch 10 (*counts as sc, ch-9*), [skip 9 sts, sc in next, ch 9] 5 times, sl st in 1st ch to join—6 sc, 6 ch-9 spaces.

Round 7: Ch 1 (*counts as 1st sc*), 9 sc in 1st ch-9 space, 10 sc in each ch-9 space around, sl st in 1st ch to join, sl st in next 4 sts— 60 sc.

Rounds 8–9: Repeat Rounds 6 and 7.

Round 10: Ch 101, [skip 9 sts, sc in next, ch 100] 5 times, sl st in 1st ch to join—6 ch-100 spaces (*hangers*).

Fasten off and weave in ends.

Finishing

Ensure long chains are neatly on sides, taking care not to tangle. Place plant into flower pot and then into Herb Holder. Gather 1 long ch at a time, until all 6 are held; adjust pot holder and plant as necessary. Ensure 2 in./5 cm hook screw is securely in place and transfer all long chains onto hook.

Harbor Placemat

Designed by Danyel Pink

Sometimes there is beauty in simplicity. This filet crochet–inspired placemat will frame your dinner dishes perfectly!

Skill Level
Easy

Finished Measurements
12 in. x 17.5 in./30.5 cm x 44.5 cm

Yarn

Knit Picks CotLin, DK weight #3 yarn (70% Tanguis cotton, 30% linen; 123 yd./112 m per 1.76 oz./50 g skein)
- 2 skeins Harbor 24464

Hook & Other Materials
- US Size F-5 (3.75 mm) crochet hook
- Yarn needle
- Blocking supplies

Gauge
17 dc and 11 rows = 4 in./10 cm
Gauge is not critical to this project.

Instructions

Ch 51.

Row 1 (RS): Dc in 4th ch from hook (*beginning ch-3 counts as dc, now and throughout*), dc in each ch across, turn—49 dc.

Row 2: Ch 3, dc in next 2, [ch 1, skip 1, dc in next] 22 times, dc in last 2, turn—27 dc, 22 ch-1 spaces.

Row 3: Ch 3, dc in next 2, ch 1, skip ch-1 space, dc in next dc, [dc in next ch-1 space, dc in next dc] 20 times, ch 1, skip ch-1 space, dc in last 3, turn—47 dc, 2 ch-1 spaces.

Row 4: Ch 3, dc in next 2, ch 1, skip ch-1 space, dc in next 3, [ch 1, skip 1, dc in next] 18 times, dc in next 2, ch 1, skip ch-1 space, dc in last 3, turn—29 dc, 20 ch-1 spaces.

Row 5: Ch 3, dc in next 2, ch 1, skip ch-1 space, dc in next 3, ch 1, skip ch-1 space, dc in next dc, [dc in next ch-1 space, dc in next dc] 16 times, [ch 1, skip ch-1 space, dc in next 3] twice, turn—45 dc, 4 ch-1 spaces.

Rows 6–37: Ch 3, dc in next 2, ch 1, skip ch-1 space, dc in next 3, ch 1, skip ch-1 space, dc in next 33, [ch 1, skip ch-1 space, dc in next 3] twice, turn—45 dc, 4 ch-1 spaces.

Row 38: Ch 3, dc in next 2, ch 1, skip ch-1 space, dc in next 3, ch 1, skip ch-1 space, dc in next, [ch 1, skip 1, dc in next] 16 times, [ch 1, skip ch-1 space, dc in next 3] twice, turn—29 dc, 20 ch-1 spaces.

Row 39: Ch 3, dc in next 2, ch 1, skip ch-1 space, dc in next 3, [dc in next ch-1 space, dc in next dc] 18 times, dc in next 2, ch 1, skip ch-1 space, dc in last 3, turn—47 dc, 2 ch-1 spaces.

Row 40: Ch 3, dc in next 2, ch 1, skip ch-1 space, dc in next, [ch 1, skip 1, dc in next] 20 times, ch 1, skip ch-1 space, dc in last 3, turn—27 dc, 22 ch-1 spaces.

Row 41: Ch 3, dc in next 2, [dc in next ch-1 space, dc in next dc] 22 times, dc in last 2, do not turn or fasten off—49 dc.

Border

Round 1: Ch 1 (*not a st*), (sc, ch 1, sc) in last dc made, rotate to work along long edge, 2 sc in each row end across, (sc, ch 1, sc) in 1st ch of starting ch, rotate to work along starting ch, sc in each ch across to last ch, (sc, ch 1, sc) in last ch, rotate to work along long edge, 2 sc in each row end across, (sc, ch 1, sc) in top of ch-3 at Row 41, rotate to work along Row 41, sc in each dc across, sl st to 1st sc to join—262 sc, 4 ch-1 corner spaces.

Round 2: Ch 3, *(dc, ch 1, dc) in corner ch-1 space, dc in each sc along side; repeat from * around, sl st to top of beginning ch-3 to join—270 dc, 4 ch-1 corner spaces.

Finishing

Fasten off and weave in ends.
Block lightly to square corners if needed.

Hexagon Centerpiece

Designed by Salena Baca

Each simple hexagon is joined at the corners as you work, building a centerpiece as you crochet each motif together. Once you get the hang of JAYGO ("join as you go"), you'll be done in no time!

Skill Level
Intermediate

Finished Measurements
Length: 23.5 in./60 cm
Width (including border): 11 in./28 cm

Yarn

Red Heart Creme de la Creme, medium weight #4 yarn (100% combed cotton; 125 yd./114 m per 2.5 oz./70.5 g skein)
- 2 skeins Linen 118

Hook & Other Materials
- US Size G-6 (4.0 mm) crochet hook
- Yarn needle

Gauge
1 motif = 3.75 in./9.5 cm
Adjust hook size if necessary to obtain gauge.

Note
- Pattern is written with join-as-you-go (JAYGO) instructions. Follow finishing notes and use chart as joining template.

Instructions

1st Motif (make 1)

Make magic ring (see "Additional Resources" on page vii for link to video tutorial).

Round 1 (RS): Ch 5 (*counts as dc, ch-2, here and throughout*), [2 dc, ch 2] 5 times in ring, dc in ring, sl st to 3rd ch of beginning ch-5 to join—12 dc, 6 ch-2 spaces.

Round 2: Sl st to 1st ch-2 space, ch 5, dc in same space, [dc in next 2 dc, (dc, ch 2, dc) in ch-2 space] 5 times, dc in next 2 dc, sl st to 3rd ch of beginning ch-5 to join—24 dc, 6 ch-2 spaces.

Round 3: Sl st to 1st ch-2 space, ch 5, dc in same space, [dc in next 4 dc, (dc, ch 2, dc) in ch-2 space] 5 times, dc in next 3 dc, sl st to 3rd ch of beginning ch-5 to join— 36 dc, 6 ch-2 spaces.

Fasten off.

Remaining Motifs (make 15)

JAYGO is worked by replacing 1 ch with a sl st to corner ch-2 space of an adjacent motif. Use chart as joining template.

Repeat Rounds 1–2 of 1st Motif.

For Motifs 2–6: JAYGO at 2 adjacent ch-2 corners forming a strip of 6 Motifs

For Motif 7: JAYGO at 3 adjacent ch-2 corners.

For Motifs 8–11: JAYGO at 4 adjacent ch-2 corners.

For Motif 12: JAYGO at 3 adjacent ch-2 corners.

For Motifs 13–16: JAYGO at 4 adjacent ch-2 corners.

Border

With RS facing, join yarn to 1st ch of Motif 7.

Round 1: Ch 5, *dc in next 8 sts, ch 2, dc in next 7 sts, skip ch-spaces, dc in next 7 sts, ch 2**; repeat from * 2 more times, ***dc in next 7 sts, skip ch-spaces, dc in next 7 sts, ch 2****; repeat from *** 2 more times, repeat from * to ** 3 times, repeat from *** to **** 2 times, dc in next 7 sts, skip ch-spaces, dc in next 7 sts, sl st to 3rd ch of beginning ch-5 to join—260 dc, 18 ch-2 spaces.

Fasten off and weave in ends.

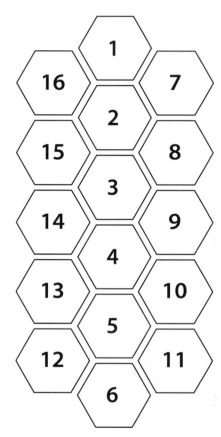

Hexagon Potholder

Designed by Salena Baca

se two contrasting colors to create this potholder in a fun, modern shape. This potholder is formed in a double layer, making it a very sturdy kitchen accessory.

Skill Level
Easy

Finished Measurements
Small: 6.5 in./16.5 cm diameter
Medium: 8 in./20 cm diameter

Yarn

Lily Sugar 'n Cream, medium weight #4 yarn (100% cotton; 120 yd./ 109.5 m per 2.5 oz./70.5 g skein in solids; 95 yd./86 m per 2 oz./56.5 g skein in variegated)
- 1 skein Teal 1133 (Color A)
- 1 skein Coral Seas Ombre 2750 (Color B)

Hook & Other Materials
- US Size H-8 (5.0 mm) crochet hook
- Yarn needle

Gauge
13 sc and 14 rows = 4 in./10 cm
Gauge is not critical to this project.

Note
- Pattern is worked twice and then seamed together to form double-layer potholder.

Instructions
Potholder Layer (make 2)

With Color A for 1st Layer, with Color B for 2nd Layer, make magic ring (see "Additional Resources" on page vii for link to video tutorial).

Round 1 (RS): Ch 1 (*not a st, here and throughout*), 6 sc in ring, sl st to 1st sc to join—6 sc.

Round 2: Ch 1, 2 sc in each st around, sl st to 1st sc to join—12 sc.

Round 3: Ch 1, [2 sc in next, sc in next] 6 times, sl st to 1st sc to join—18 sc.

Round 4: Ch 1, [2 sc in next, sc in next 2] 6 times, sl st to 1st sc to join—24 sc.

Round 5: Ch 1, [2 sc in next, sc in next 3] 6 times, sl st to 1st sc to join—30 sc.

Round 6: Ch 1, [2 sc in next, sc in next 4] 6 times, sl st to 1st sc to join—36 sc.

Round 7: Ch 1, [2 sc in next, sc in next 5] 6 times, sl st to 1st sc to join—42 sc.

Round 8: Ch 1, [2 sc in next, sc in next 6] 6 times, sl st to 1st sc to join—48 sc.

Round 9: Ch 1, [2 sc in next, sc in next 7] 6 times, sl st to 1st sc to join—54 sc.

Round 10: Ch 1, [2 sc in next, sc in next 8] 6 times, sl st to 1st sc to join—60 sc.

Fasten off for Small, continue for Medium.

Round 11: Ch 1, [2 sc in next, sc in next 9] 6 times, sl st to 1st sc to join—66 sc.

Round 12: Ch 1, [2 sc in next, sc in next 10] 6 times, sl st to 1st sc to join—72 sc.

Round 13: Ch 1, [2 sc in next, sc in next 11] 6 times, sl st to 1st sc to join—78 sc.

Fasten off.

Finishing (all sizes)

Hold Layers 1 and 2 together (RS facing outward). With Color B Layer facing, join Color A to last round in BLO of both thicknesses at seam, ch 12 (*loop made*), sl st in same st of last round, BLO sl st loosely through both thicknesses around, sl st to 1st st to join—60 (78) sl sts, 1 ch-12 space. Fasten off and weave in all ends.

Nana's Garden Trivet

Designed by Danyel Pink

Protect your counters and tables from hot pots and casseroles with this beautiful, mandala-inspired trivet.

Skill Level
Intermediate

Finished Measurements
Approx. 8 in./20 cm diameter; fits 7 in./17.5 cm cork trivet

Yarn

Lily Sugar 'n Cream, worsted weight #4 yarn (100% cotton; 120 yd./ 109.5 m per 2.5 oz./70.5 g ball)
- 1 ball White 0010 (Color A)
- 1 ball Robin's Egg 1215 (Color B)
- 1 ball Hot Pink 1740 (Color C)

Hook & Other Materials
- US Size G-6 (4.0 mm) crochet hook
- 7 in./17.5 cm circular cork trivet (optional)
- Stitch marker
- Yarn needle

Gauge
11 hdc and 6 rows = 2 in./5 cm
Adjust hook size if necessary to obtain gauge. If not using cork trivet, gauge is not critical.

Special Stitches
3-dc cl (3 double crochet cluster) = Yo, insert hook in indicated space, yo and pull up loop, yo and pull through 2 loops on hook, [yo, insert hook in same space, yo and pull up loop, yo and pull through 2 loops on hook] 2 times, yo and pull through all 4 loops on hook.
4-dc cl (4 double crochet cluster) = Yo, insert hook in indicated space, yo and pull up loop, yo and pull through 2 loops on hook, [yo, insert hook in same space, yo and pull up loop, yo and pull through 2 loops on hook] 3 times, yo and pull through all 5 loops on hook.
5-dc cl (5 double crochet cluster) = Yo, insert hook in indicated space, yo and pull up loop, yo and pull through 2 loops on hook, [yo, insert

hook in same space, yo and pull up loop, yo and pull through 2 loops on hook] 4 times, yo and pull through all 6 loops on hook.

V-st (V-stitch) = (Dc, ch 2, dc) in indicated st.

Notes

- Ch-1 at the beginning of a round does not count as a st.
- Trivet is worked in two layers and can be made without the cork trivet insert.
- Bottom of Trivet is worked in a continuous spiral; use stitch marker to keep track of sts.
- To "join with a sc," put yarn on hook, insert hook into indicated st and pull up loop, yo and pull through both loops on hook to complete sc.

Instructions

Bottom Layer

With any color, make magic ring (see "Additional Resources" on page vii for link to video tutorial).

Round 1: Ch 1, 12 hdc in ring—12 hdc.

Round 2: 2 hdc in each st around—24 hdc.

Round 3: [Hdc in next, 2 hdc in next] 12 times—36 hdc.

Round 4: [Hdc in next 2, 2 hdc in next] 12 times—48 hdc.

Round 5: [Hdc in next 3, 2 hdc in next] 12 times—60 hdc.

Round 6: [Hdc in next 4, 2 hdc in next] 12 times—72 hdc.

Round 7: [Hdc in next 5, 2 hdc in next] 12 times—84 hdc.

Round 8: [Hdc in next 6, 2 hdc in next] 12 times—96 hdc.

Round 9: [Hdc in next 7, 2 hdc in next] 12 times—108 hdc.

Round 10: [Hdc in next 8, 2 hdc in next] 12 times, sc in next st—120 sts. Fasten off.

Top Layer

With Color A, make magic ring.

Round 1: Ch 4 (*counts as dc, ch-1*), [dc in ring, ch 1] 8 times, sl st to 3rd ch of beginning ch-4—9 dc, 9 ch-1 spaces. Fasten off Color A.

Round 2: Join Color B with sl st in any ch-1 space, ch 2, 3-dc cl in same space, ch 2, [4-dc cl in next ch-1 space, ch 2] 8 times, sl st to top of 1st cluster—9 cl, 9 ch-2 spaces. Fasten off Color B.

Round 3: Join Color C with a sc in any ch-2 space, 3 sc in same space, 4 sc in each ch-2 space around, sl st to 1st sc—27 sc. Fasten off Color C.

Round 4: Join Color A with sl st in BL of any sc, ch 5 (*counts as dc, ch-2*), dc in same st, skip 2 sc, [V-st in BL of next sc, skip 2 sc] 11 times, sl st to 3rd ch of beginning ch-5—12 V-sts. Fasten off Color A.

Round 5: Join Color B with sl st in any ch-2 space, ch 2, 4-dc cl in same space, ch 4, [5-dc cl in next ch-2 space, ch 4] 11 times, sl st to top of 1st cluster—12 cl, 12 ch-4 spaces. Fasten off Color B.

Round 6: Join Color C with a sc in any ch-4 space, 5 sc in same space, 6 sc in each ch-4 space around, sl st to 1st sc—72 sc. Fasten off Color C.

Round 7: Join Color A with sl st in BL of any 2nd sc of 6-sc group, ch 5 (*counts as dc, ch-2*), dc in same st, skip 2 sc, [V-st in BL of next sc, skip 2 sc] 23 times, sl st to 3rd ch of beginning ch-5—24 V-sts. Fasten off Color A.

Round 8: Join Color B with sl st in any ch-2 space, ch 2, 4-dc cl in same space, ch 4, [5-dc cl in next ch-2 space, ch 4] 23 times, sl st to top of 1st cl—24 cl, 24 ch-4 spaces. Fasten off Color B.

Round 9: Join Color C with a sc in any ch-4 space, 4 sc in same space, 5 sc in each ch-4 space around, sl st to 1st sc—120 sc. Do not fasten off.

Assembly

Weave in ends of Top Layer before continuing.
Hold wrong sides of Top Layer and Bottom Layer together.

Insert hook through BL of next st on Top Layer and then through BL (*loop closest to you*) of any st on Bottom Layer, and sl st to join. Sl st through BL on last round of Top and Bottom Layers evenly around. When half the circle has been joined, insert cork trivet (*optional*) and then continue stitching Layers together. After last sl st is made, cut yarn, thread tail from front to back under both loops of next stitch and back down through same stitch where tail began to form invisible join (see "Additional Resources" on page vii for link to video tutorial). Fasten off and weave in end securely.

Puffy Dishcloth

Designed by Emily Truman

Form and function meet bright-colored puff stitches. Make one in every color!

Skill Level
Intermediate

Finished Measurements
8.5 x 9 in./21.5 cm x 23 cm

Yarn

Lion Brand Kitchen Cotton, worsted weight #4 yarn (100% cotton;
99 yd./90 m per 2 oz./56.5 g skein)
• 2 skeins Tropic Breeze 148 (Citrus 157, Snap Pea 130, and Cayenne
114 also pictured)

Hook & Other Materials
• US Size 7 (4.5 mm) crochet hook
• Yarn needle

Gauge
Gauge is not critical to this project.

Special Stitches
3-tr cl (3-treble cluster) = *Yo twice and insert hook in indicated st, [yo and
pull through 2 loops] twice; repeat from * 2 more times in same st, yo
and pull through all loops on hook.

Instructions

Ch 32.

Row 1 (RS): Sc in 2nd ch from hook and in each ch across, turn—31 sc.

Row 2: Ch 1, sc in each st across, turn.

Row 3: Ch 1, sc in next 3, *3-tr cl in next, sc in next 3; repeat from * across, turn—7 cl, 24 sc.

Rows 4–6: Ch 1, sc in each st across, turn.

Row 7: Ch 1, sc in next 5, *3-tr cl in next, sc in next 3; repeat from * across to last 2, sc in last 2, turn—6 cl, 25 sc.

Rows 8–10: Ch 1, sc in each st across, turn.

Rows 11–34: Repeat Rows 3–10 three times.

Rows 35–37: Repeat Rows 3–5.

Fasten off.

Border

With RS (cluster side) facing, ch 1, sc evenly around entire dishcloth, working 3 sc in each corner, before joining, ch 12, sc in same st as 1st sc, turn, sl st in next 12 chs, sl st to join round in next st.

Fasten off and weave in ends.

Superstar Coasters

Designed by Danyel Pink

Whip up a set of these cute coasters in any combination of colors. They'll protect your furniture from spills and scratches, and they make a great gift, too!

Skill Level
Easy

Finished Measurements
5 in./12.5 cm wide

Yarn

Lily Sugar 'n Cream, worsted weight #4 yarn (100% cotton; 120 yd./ 109.5 m per 2.5 oz./70.5 g skein)
- 1 skein White 1 (Color A)
- 1 skein Robin's Egg 1215 (Color B)

Hook & Other Materials
- US Size H-8 (5.0 mm) crochet hook
- Yarn needle

Gauge
Gauge is not critical to this project.

Special Stitch
Picot = Ch 3, sl st in 3rd ch from hook.

Instructions

With Color A, make magic ring (see "Additional Resources" on page vii for link to video tutorial).

Round 1: Ch 3 (*counts as dc*), dc in ring, ch 1, [2 dc in ring, ch 1] 4 times, join with sl st to 3rd ch of beginning ch-3—10 dc, 5 ch-1 spaces.

Round 2: Sl st in next dc, sl st in ch-1 space, ch 5, *sl st in next ch-1 space, ch 5; repeat from * 3 more times, join with sl st at base of beginning ch-5—5 ch-5 spaces, 5 sl st.

Round 3: *(3 sc, ch 1, 3 sc) in next ch-5 space, sl st in ch-1 space from Round 1; repeat from * around—30 sc, 5 ch-1 spaces. Fasten off Color A.

Round 4: Join Color B with sl st to any ch-1 space, *ch 3, skip 3 sts, dc in sl st, ch 3, skip 3 sts, sl st in next ch-1 space; repeat from * around, working last sl st in 1st ch of first ch-3 space—10 ch-3 spaces, 5 dc, 5 sl st.

Round 5: Ch 1 (*not a st*), 4 sc in ch-3 space, 4 sc in next ch-3 space, ch 1, *[4 sc in next ch-3 space] twice, ch 1; repeat from * around, join with sl st to 1st sc—40 sc, 5 ch-1 spaces.

Round 6: Ch 1 (*not a st*), *sc in next 8, 3 sc in ch-1 space; repeat from * around, join with sl st to 1st sc—55 sc.

Round 7: Ch 1 (*not a st*), *sc in next 9, sl st in next, Picot, sc in next; repeat from * around, join with sl st to 1st sc—50 sc, 5 Picot. Fasten off Color B.

Weave in all ends.

Windsor Dishcloth

Designed by Danyel Pink

Handmade dishcloths have a variety of uses around the home. The colors and texture of this cloth are sure to make it your new favorite!

Skill Level
Intermediate

Finished Measurements
8.5 x 8.5 in./21.5 x 21.5 cm

Yarn

Peaches & Creme, worsted weight #4 yarn (100% cotton; 120 yd./109.5 m per 2.5 oz./70.5 g ball)
- 1 ball Ocean Coral 11714 (Color A)
- 1 ball Gold 11605 (Color B)

Hook & Other Materials
- US Size H-8 (5.0 mm) crochet hook
- Yarn needle

Gauge
7 sts and 6 rows = 2 in./5 cm
Gauge is not critical to this project.

Notes
- A ch-1 at the beginning of a row does not count as a st.
- Keep tr sts to RS of work by crocheting them in front of previous 2 rows.
- Change colors by completing last pull-through of hdc at end of even-numbered rows with new color. Do not fasten off at each color change; carry unused yarn along side of work (see "Additional Resources" on page vii for link to video tutorial).

Instructions

With Color A, ch 28.

Row 1 (RS): Sc in 2nd ch from hook, [ch 1, skip 1, sc in next 3] 6 times, ch 1, skip 1, sc in last—20 sc, 7 ch-1 spaces.

Row 2: Ch 1, turn, hdc in each st and ch-1 space across, change to Color B—27 hdc.

Row 3: Ch 1, turn, sc in 1st, tr in skipped st 3 rows below, [sc in next, ch 1, skip 1, sc in next, tr in skipped st 3 rows below] 6 times, sc in last—7 tr, 6 ch-1 spaces, 14 sc.

Row 4: Ch 1, turn, hdc in each st and ch-1 space across, change to Color A—27 hdc.

Row 5: Ch 1, turn, sc in 1st, ch 1, skip 1, sc in next, [tr in skipped st 3 rows below, sc in next, ch 1, skip 1, sc in next] 6 times—6 tr, 7 ch-1 spaces, 14 sc.

Row 6: Ch 1, turn, hdc in each st and ch-1 space across, change to Color B—27 hdc.

Rows 7–24: Repeat Rows 3–6 four times, and then repeat Rows 3–4 once more. Fasten off Color B.

Row 25: Ch 1, turn, sc in next 3, [tr in skipped st 3 rows below, sc in next 3] 6 times, do not fasten off or turn. Continue to Trim.

Trim

With RS facing, rotate cloth to begin working along side.

Round 1: 2 sc in same corner st, work 23 sc evenly across side, 3 sc in corner, sc in next 25 across bottom, 3 sc in corner, 23 sc evenly across side, 3 sc in corner, sc in next 25 across top, ch 1, sl st to corner sc to join.

Finishing

Fasten off and weave in all ends.
Cloth may slant slightly; block square if desired.

Living

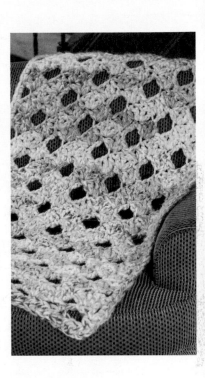

Falling Leaves Wall Tapestry

Designed by Salena Baca

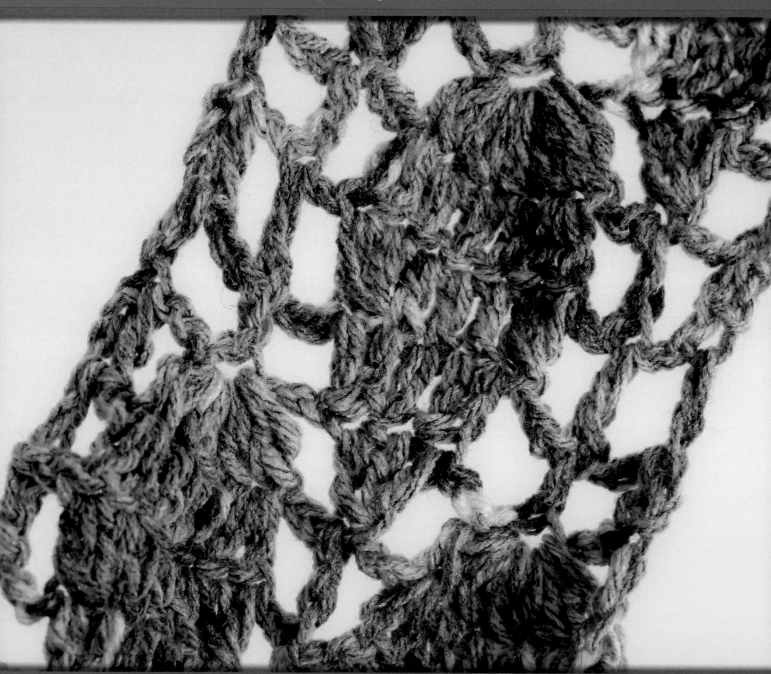

Just like macramé, crochet pattern work can create beautiful wall-hangings and decor! Complete this design with any variety of yarn, and play with color and texture for a fun, daring look.

Skill Level
Intermediate

Finished Measurements
Width: 7 in./17.5 cm
Length (without tassel): 15 in./38 cm

Yarn

Red Heart Super Saver, medium weight #4 yarn (100% acrylic; 236 yd./ 215 m per 5 oz./142 g skein)
• 1 skein Soapstone 3976

Hook & Other Materials
• US Size I-9 (5.5 mm) crochet hook
• 12 in./30.5 cm dowel, or natural twig
• Yarn needle
• 5 in./12.5 cm square cardboard (for tassel)

Special Stitches
2-dc Cl (2 double crochet cluster) = [Yo, insert hook in st, yo and pull up loop, yo and pull through 2 loops on hook] twice in same st, yo and pull through all 3 loops on hook.
dc2tog (double crochet 2 together) = [Yo, insert hook in next st, yo and pull up loop, yo and pull through 2 loops on hook] twice, yo and pull through all 3 loops on hook.
dc3tog (double crochet 3 together) = [Yo, insert hook in next st, yo and pull up loop, yo and pull through 2 loops on hook] 3 times, yo and pull through all 4 loops on hook.
dc5tog (double crochet 5 together) = [Yo, insert hook in next st, yo and pull up loop, yo and pull through 2 loops on hook] 5 times, yo and pull through all 6 loops on hook.

Gauge

12 dc and 5.5 rows = 4 in./10 cm
Gauge is not critical to this project.

Note

- Beginning ch-2 of each row does not count as a st.

Instructions

Ch 21.

Row 1 (RS): Dc in 3rd ch from hook, ch 3, skip 3 sts, 5 2-dc Cl in next, ch 3, skip 3 sts, dc3tog, ch 3, skip 3 sts, 5 2-dc Cl in next, ch 3, skip 3 sts, dc in last—13 sts, 4 ch-3 spaces.

Row 2: Ch 2, turn, dc in dc, *ch 2, skip 3 ch, 2 dc in next, dc in next 3, 2 dc in next, ch 2, skip 3 ch, dc in next; repeat from * once more—17 dc, 4 ch-2 spaces.

Row 3: Ch 2, turn, dc in dc, *ch 3, skip 2 ch, dc2tog, dc in next 3, dc2tog, ch 3, skip 2 ch, dc in next; repeat from * once more—13 sts, 4 ch-3 spaces.

Row 4: Ch 2, turn, dc in dc, *ch 3, skip 3 ch, dc2tog, dc in next, dc2tog, ch 3, skip 3 ch, dc in next; repeat from * once more—9 sts, 4 ch-3 spaces.

Row 5: Ch 2, turn, dc in dc, ch 3, skip 3 ch, dc3tog, ch 3, skip 3 ch, 5 2-dc Cl in next, ch 3, skip 3 ch, dc3tog, ch 3, skip 3 ch, dc in next—9 sts, 4 ch-3 spaces.

Row 6: Ch 2, turn, dc in dc, ch 2, skip 3 ch, dc in next, ch 2, skip 3 ch, 2 dc in next, dc in next 3, 2 dc in next, ch 2, skip 3 ch, dc in next, ch 2, skip 3 ch, dc in next—11 sts, 4 ch-2 spaces.

Row 7: Ch 2, turn, dc in dc, ch 3, skip 2 ch, dc in next, ch 3, skip 2 ch, dc2tog, dc in next 3, dc2tog, ch 3, skip 2 ch, dc in next, ch 3, skip 2 ch, dc in next—9 sts, 4 ch-3 spaces.

Row 8: Ch 2, turn, dc in dc, ch 3, skip 3 ch, dc in next, ch 3, skip 3 ch, dc2tog, dc in next, dc2tog, ch 3, skip 3 ch, dc in next, ch 3, skip 3 ch, dc in next—7 sts, 4 ch-3 spaces.

Row 9: Ch 2, turn, dc in dc, ch 3, skip 3 ch, 5 2-dc Cl in next, ch 3, skip 3 ch, dc3tog, ch 3, skip 3 ch, 5 2-dc Cl in next, ch 3, skip 3 ch, dc in next—13 sts, 4 ch-3 spaces.

Rows 10–16: Repeat Rows 2–8.

Row 17: Ch 2, turn, dc in dc, ch 3, skip 3 ch, dc in next, ch 3, skip 3 ch, dc3tog, ch 3, skip 3 ch, dc in next, ch 3, skip 3 ch, dc in next—5 sts, 4 ch-3 spaces.

Row 18: Ch 2, turn, dc in dc, [ch 2, skip 3 ch, dc in next] 4 times—5 dc, 4 ch-2 spaces.

Row 19: Ch 2, turn, dc in dc, [ch 1, skip 2 ch, dc in next] 4 times—5 dc, 4 ch-1 spaces.

Row 20: Ch 2, turn, dc in dc, [skip 1 ch, dc in next] 4 times—5 dc.

Row 21: Ch 2, turn, dc5tog, ch 1 to secure st, fasten off—1 dc5tog.

Attach Tapestry to Dowel

Hold Tapestry in center of 12 in./30.5 cm dowel. With 24 in./61 cm length of yarn and yarn needle, whip-stitch foundation ch to dowel, fasten off on each end to secure.

Hanger

Cut 30 in./76 cm piece of yarn, and fasten ends evenly to dowel at both sides of Tapestry at foundation ch.

Tassel

Fold 24 in./61 cm piece of yarn in half, draw through dc5tog on last row of Tapestry, ensure both sides of yarn are even, tie a knot.

With 5 in./12.5 cm piece of square cardboard, wrap yarn around 50 times. Cut on one side to create bundle of yarn for tassel.

Place bundle of yarn evenly between tails at end of tapestry, and secure with another knot. Wrap tails evenly around bundle 1 in./2.5 cm below end of tapestry, and tie another knot to form tassel.

Trim bundle ends evenly.

Fast-Track Basket

Designed by Salena Baca

Super bulky yarn is very durable and sturdy, perfect for storage solutions. Use one entire skein of Fast-Track to make this basket to hold toys, yarn, towels, gifts, and more!

Skill Level
Intermediate

Finished Measurements
Diameter: 10.5 in./27 cm
Circumference: 28 in./71 cm

Yarn

Lion Brand Fast-Track, super bulky weight #6 yarn (60% cotton, 40% polyester; 149 yd./136 m per 8 oz./227 g skein)
• 1 skein Go Kart Green 130

Hook & Other Materials
• US Size L-11 (8.0 mm) crochet hook
• Yarn needle

Gauge
10 sts and 8 rows = 4 in./10 cm
Adjust hook size if necessary to obtain gauge.

Instructions

Make magic ring (see "Additional Resources" on page vii for link to video tutorial).

Round 1 (RS): Ch 1 (*not a stitch, here and throughout*), 6 sc in ring, sl st to join—6 sc.

Round 2: Ch 1, 2 sc in each st around, sl st to join—12 sc.

Round 3: Ch 1, [2 sc in next, sc in next] 6 times, sl st to join—18 sc.

Round 4: Ch 1, [2 sc in next, sc in next 2] 6 times, sl st to join—24 sc.

Round 5: Ch 1, [2 sc in next, sc in next 3] 6 times, sl st to join—30 sc.

Round 6: Ch 1, [2 sc in next, sc in next 4] 6 times, sl st to join—36 sc.

Round 7: Ch 1, [2 sc in next, sc in next 5] 6 times, sl st to join—42 sc.

Round 8: Ch 1, [2 sc in next, sc in next 6] 6 times, sl st to join—48 sc.

Round 9: Ch 1, [2 sc in next, sc in next 7] 6 times, sl st to join—54 sc.

Round 10: Ch 1, [2 sc in next, sc in next 8] 6 times, sl st to join—60 sc.

Round 11: Ch 1, [2 sc in next, sc in next 9] 6 times, sl st to join—66 sc.

Round 12: Ch 1, [2 sc in next, sc in next 10] 6 times, sl st to join—72 sc.

Round 13: Ch 1, BLO sc in each st around, sl st to join.

Round 14: Ch 1, sc in each st around, sl st to join.

Round 15: Ch 1, sc in next 2, [ch 2, skip 2, dc in next, ch 2, skip 2, sc in next 3] 8 times, ch 2, skip 2, dc, ch 2, skip 2, sc in last, sl st to join—72 sts.

Round 16: Ch 1, sc in each st around, sl st to join.

Round 17: Ch 5 (*counts as dc, ch-2*), skip 2, [sc in next 3, ch 2, skip 2, dc in next, ch 2, skip 2] 8 times, sc in next 3, ch 2, skip 2, sl st to join—72 sts.

Round 18: Ch 1, sc in each st around, sl st to join.

Rounds 19–24: Repeat Rounds 15–18 once and then Rounds 15–16 once.

Round 25: Ch 20, skip 12, sc in next 24, ch 20, skip 12, sc in next 24, sl st to join—48 sc, 2 ch-20 spaces.

Round 26: [Sc in next 20 chs, sl st in next 24 sc] twice, sl st to join—40 sc, 48 sl sts.

Fasten off and weave in ends.

Fast-Track Rug

Designed by *Salena Baca*

This bulky fabric yarn works up quickly, creating a decorative rug that complements a space while giving you a comfy place to stand!

Skill Level
Intermediate

Finished Measurements
Width: 20 in./51 cm
Length (including border): 14.5 in./37 cm

Yarn

Lion Brand Fast-Track, super bulky weight #6 yarn (60% cotton, 40% polyester; 149 yd./136 m per 8 oz./227 g skein)
- 1 skein Dune Buggy Denim 108 (Color A)
- 1 skein Chopper Grey 149 (Color B)

Hook & Other Materials
- US Size L-11 (8.0 mm) crochet hook
- Yarn needle

Gauge
10 sts and 8 rows = 4 in./10 cm
Adjust hook size if necessary to obtain gauge.

Note
- Pattern can be adjusted in multiples of 8 + 3 (+1 for starting chain), repeat Rows 2–5 as desired.

Instructions

With Color A, ch 44.

Row 1 (RS): Sc in 2nd ch from hook and in each ch across, turn—43 sc.

Row 2: Ch 1 (*not a st, here and throughout*), [sc in next 3, ch 2, skip 2, dc in next, ch 2, skip 2] 5 times, sc in last 3, turn—43 sts.

Row 3: Ch 1, sc in each st across, turn.

Rows 4: Ch 6 (*counts as dc, ch-3*), skip 3 sts, [sc in next 3, ch 2, skip 2, dc in next, ch 2, skip 2] 4 times, ch 3, skip 3 sts, dc in last, turn—43 sts.

Row 5: Ch 1, sc in each st across, turn.

Rows 6–27: Repeat Rows 2–5, ending on a repeat of Row 3.

Fasten off.

Border

With RS of Rug facing, attach Color B to end of Row 3.

Round 1 (RS): Ch 1, 2 sc in same, 2 sc in every other row end across side, (sc, ch 1, sc) in 1st sc of Row 27, *skip 1 st, 2 sc in next**; repeat from * across Row 27, (sc, ch1, sc) in last sc of Row 27, skip 2 row ends on side, 2 sc in next, 2 sc in every other row end across side, (sc, ch 1, sc) in last st of Row 1, repeat from * to ** across Row 1, (sc, ch 1, sc) in 1st sc of Row 1, sl st to 1st sc to join—102 sc, 4 ch-1 spaces.

Round 2: Ch 1, sc in each st around working (sc, ch 1, sc) in each ch-1 corner space, sl st to 1st sc to join.

Fasten off and weave in all ends.

Nebula Pillow

Designed by Danyel Pink

T his gorgeous pillow is the perfect addition to your home decor. It will look fabulous in your bedroom or living room!

Skill Level
Intermediate

Finished Measurements
Fits 16 in./40.5 cm square pillow

Yarn

Knit Picks Bare Preciosa, worsted weight #4 yarn (100% merino; 273 yd./ 250 m per 3.5 oz./100 g hank)
 • 2 hanks Bare 26716 (Color A)
Knit Picks Preciosa Tonal, worsted weight #4 yarn (100% merino; 273 yd./ 250 m per 3.5 oz./100 g hank)
 • 1 hank Blue Skies 26724 (Color B)

Hook & Other Materials
 • US Size J-10 (6.0 mm) crochet hook
 • Six 1 in./2.5 cm buttons
 • Tape measure
 • Stitch markers
 • Yarn needle

Gauge
14 sts = 4 in./10 cm; stitch height not critical.
Adjust hook size if necessary to obtain gauge.

Notes
 • A ch-1 at the beginning of a row does not count as a st.
 • When working sl st rows, keep an even tension to prevent bunching and to make sts easier to work into.
 • Pillow Case is worked in rows and then seamed along two sides.
 • Front Flap is worked in rows and then sewn to top edge of Pillow Case, forming an "envelope." Front Flap can be blocked if necessary to straighten/lengthen the flat edge.
 • Buttons are added last, and can be positioned as desired to stretch the points of the flap.

Instructions

Pillow Case

With Color A, ch 57 (*or until ch measures width of pillow*).

Row 1 (RS): Hdc in 2nd ch from hook and in each ch across—56 sts.

Rows 2–3: Ch 1, turn, hdc in each hdc across.

Row 4: Ch 1, turn, sl st in BL of each hdc across.

Rows 5–6: Ch 1, turn, sl st in BL of each sl st across.

Row 7: Ch 1, turn, hdc in BL of each sl st across.

Rows 8–9: Ch 1, turn, hdc in each hdc across.

Repeat Rows 4–9 until piece measures 33 in./84 cm (*or just over twice the height of pillow*). Additional rows may be necessary for fluffier pillows.

Fasten off, leaving a 20 in./51 cm tail for seaming.

Fold Pillow Case in half, aligning rows of hdc and sl sts. With needle and long tail, whipstitch side of Pillow Case together.

Cut 20 in./51 cm length of yarn. Whipstitch other side of Pillow Case together. Leave top open.

Front Flap

Note: If making custom size, work instructions until flat edge of half-circle is approximately the same size as the open edge of Case, ending with an even-numbered row, and then continue to Round 19.

With Color B, make magic ring (see "Additional Resources" on page vii for link to video tutorial).

Row 1: Ch 3 (*counts as dc*), 6 dc in ring, turn—7 dc.

Row 2: Ch 4 (*counts as dc, ch 1*), dc in next dc, *ch 1, dc in next; repeat from * across, turn—6 ch-1 spaces.

Row 3 (RS): Ch 1, sc in same st, *(sc, hdc, sc) in next ch-1 space; repeat from * across, sc in 3rd ch of ch-4, turn—6 groups of 3 sts.

Note: Sts worked into ch-spaces will be referred to as "groups" from now on.

Row 4: Ch 1, sc in same st, *ch 3, sc between next 2 groups; repeat from * 4 more times, ch 3, skip last group, sc in last sc, turn—6 ch-3 spaces.

Row 5: Ch 1, sc in same st, *(sc, 2 hdc, sc) in next ch-3 space; repeat from * across, sc in last sc, turn—6 groups of 4 sts.

Row 6: Ch 1, sc in same st, *ch 4, sc between next 2 groups; repeat from * 4 more times, ch 4, skip last group, sc in last sc, turn—6 ch-4 spaces.

Row 7: Ch 1, sc in same st, *(sc, 3 hdc, sc) in next ch-4 space; repeat from * across, sc in last sc, turn—6 groups of 5 sts.

Row 8: Ch 1, sc in same st, *ch 5, sc between next 2 groups; repeat from * 4 more times, ch 5, skip last group, sc in last sc, turn—6 ch-5 spaces.

Row 9: Ch 1, sc in same st, *(sc, 4 hdc, sc) in next ch-5 space; repeat from * across, sc in last sc, turn—6 groups of 6 sts.

Row 10: Ch 1, sc in same st, *ch 6, sc between next 2 groups; repeat from * 4 more times, ch 6, skip last group, sc in last sc, turn—6 ch-6 spaces.

Row 11: Ch 1, sc in same st, *(sc, 5 hdc, sc) in next ch-6 space; repeat from * across, sc in last sc, turn—6 groups of 7 sts.

Row 12: Ch 1, sc in same st, *ch 7, sc between next 2 groups; repeat from * 4 more times, ch 7, skip last group, sc in last sc, turn—6 ch-7 spaces.

Row 13: Ch 1, sc in same st, *(sc, 6 hdc, sc) in next ch-7 space; repeat from * across, sc in last sc, turn—6 groups of 8 sts.

Row 14: Ch 1, sc in same st, *ch 8, sc between next 2 groups; repeat from * 4 more times, ch 8, skip last group, sc in last sc, turn—6 ch-8 spaces.

Row 15: Ch 1, sc in same st, *(sc, 7 hdc, sc) in next ch-8 space; repeat from * across, sc in last sc, turn—6 groups of 9 sts.

Row 16: Ch 1, sc in same st, *ch 9, sc between next 2 groups; repeat from * 4 more times, ch 9, skip last group, sc in last sc, turn—6 ch-9 spaces.

Row 17: Ch 1, sc in same st, *(sc, 8 hdc, sc) in next ch-9 space; repeat from * across, sc in last sc, turn—6 groups of 10 sts.

Row 18: Ch 1, sc in same st, *ch 10, sc between next 2 groups; repeat from * 4 more times, ch 10, skip last group, sc in last sc, turn—6 ch-10 spaces.

Round **19:** Ch 1, sc in same st, *(sc, 4 hdc, dc, ch 5, sl st in top of dc, 4 hdc, sc) in next ch-10 space; repeat from * across, sc in last sc, ch 1, do not turn, rotate piece to work into ends of rows along flat edge, hdc evenly across, ch 1, sl st to 1st sc to join. Fasten off, leaving a 20 in./51 cm tail for sewing.

Finishing

With RS facing each other, line up flat edge of Front Flap with one open edge of Pillow Case. Use stitch markers to hold ends and middle in position. With needle and long tail, whipstitch Flap onto Case, forming an "envelope."

Weave in all ends.

Put pillow into Case. Stretch groups from Round 19 to form star shape. With needle and yarn, sew buttons into place (*use photo as guide*), and then fasten buttons using ch-5 loops.

(Sweet) Dreamcatcher

Designed by Emily Truman

This dreamcatcher only catches sweet dreams of yarn, crochet hooks, and uninterrupted counting.

Skill Level
Intermediate

Finished Measurements
Diameter: 8 in./20 cm

Yarn
Knit Picks Chroma Fingering, fingering weight #1 yarn (70% superwash wool, 30% nylon; 396 yd./362 m per 3.5 oz./100 g skein)
• 1 skein Hollyhock 26543

Hook & Other Materials
• US Size G-6 (4.0 mm) crochet hook
• Yarn needle
• 8 in./20 cm embroidery hoop
• 3 ft./91 cm leather lace, 0.125 in./0.3 cm wide
• Pony beads in matching colors
• 6 feathers in matching colors

Gauge
See "gauge check" following round 5 below.
Adjust hook size if necessary to obtain gauge.

Special Stitches
2-dc Cl (2 double crochet cluster) = [Yo and insert hook in next st, yo and pull up loop, yo and pull through 2 loops] 2 times in same st, yo and pull through all loops on hook.
3-dc Cl (3 double crochet cluster) = [Yo and insert hook in next st, yo and pull up loop, yo and pull through 2 loops] 3 times in same st, yo and pull through all loops on hook.

Note
• Beginning ch-1 does not count as a st.

Instructions

Make magic ring (see "Additional Resources" on page vii for link to video tutorial).

Round 1: Ch 1, 6 sc in ring, join—6 sc.

Round 2: Ch 1, *sc in next, ch 1; repeat from * around, join—6 sc, 6 ch-1 spaces.

Round 3: Sl st to 1st ch-1 space, ch 3 (*counts as 1st dc*), (dc, ch 2, 2 dc) in same, (2 dc, ch 2, 2 dc) in each ch-1 space around, sl st to 3rd ch of beginning ch-3 to join—24 dc, 6 ch-2 spaces.

Round 4: Ch 1, sc in space between last dc and beginning ch-3, *ch 4, sc in next ch-2 space, ch 4**, skip 2 dc, sc in space before next dc; repeat from * around, ending last repeat at **, sl st to 1st sc to join—12 sc, 12 ch-4 spaces.

Round 5: Ch 3, 2-dc Cl in same (*counts as 3-dc Cl*), ch 4, *sl st in next sc, ch 4**, 3-dc Cl in next sc, ch 4; repeat from * around, ending last repeat at **, sl st to top of 1st cluster to join—6 clusters, 12 ch-4 spaces.

Gauge check: 3½ in./9 cm from point to point.

Round 6: *[Ch 3, tr in ch-4 space 2 rounds down] twice, ch 3, sl st in 3-dc Cl; repeat from * around, last sl st serves as join—12 tr, 18 ch-3 spaces.

Round 7: Ch 3, 2-dc Cl in same (*counts as 3-dc Cl*), *ch 3, sc in next ch-3 space, ch 3, 3-dc Cl in next ch-3 space, ch 3, sc in next ch-3 space, ch 3**, 3-dc Cl in next sl st; repeat from * around, ending last repeat at **, sl st to top of 1st cluster to join—12 clusters, 24 ch-3 spaces.

Round 8: *Ch 3, tr in ch-3 space 2 rounds down (*directly over sc from previous round*), ch 3, sl st in 3-dc Cl; repeat from * around, last sl st serves as join—12 tr, 24 ch-3 spaces.

Round 9: Sl st in next ch-3 space, ch 1, hdc in same space, ch 6, *hdc in next ch-3 space, ch 6; repeat from * around, sl st to 1st hdc to join—24 hdc, 24 ch-6 spaces.

Round 10: Working around hoop with each st, *ch 1, 14 sc in next ch-6 space; repeat from * around, sl st to 1st sc to join—336 sc.

Fasten off and weave in ends.

Assembly

Cut 3 lengths of leather approx. 9 in./23 cm long. Fold 1 piece in half, weave through a space in last round and secure by pulling ends through loop. Skip 1 space on last round and repeat for second length of leather. Skip 1 more space and repeat for last length. Place beads as desired on ends of leather and knot to secure. Place end of each feather through pony beads. Ensure that they are held tightly. If feather is too loose, craft glue can be used to secure.

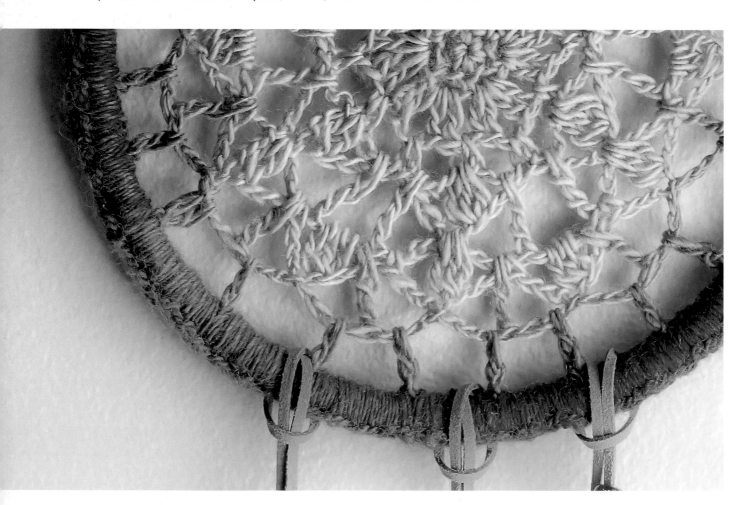

Trellis Blanket

Designed by Emily Truman

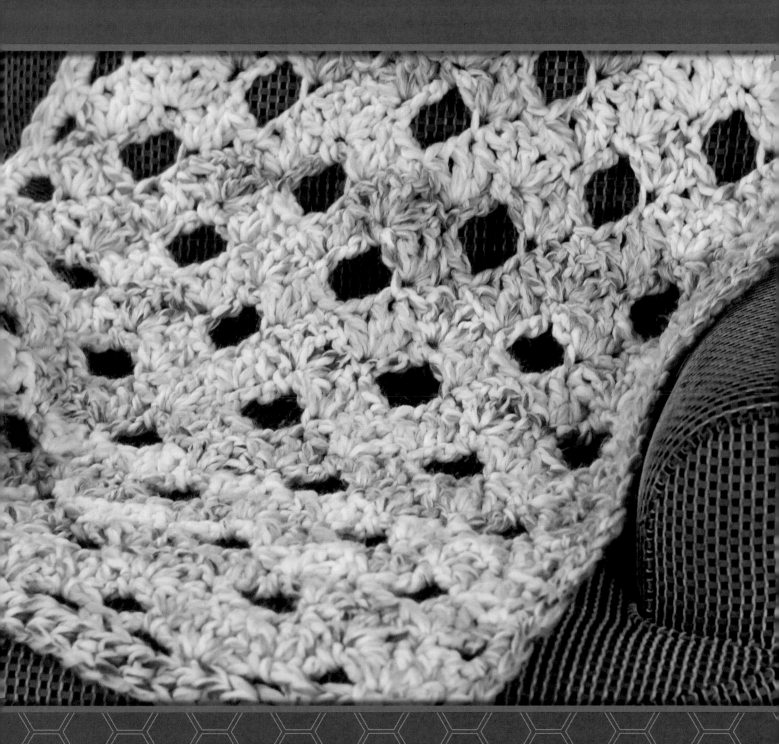

J umbo yarn makes this a quick throw, ready to place at the end of a bed.

Skill Level
Easy

Finished Measurements
Length: 56 in./142 cm
Width: 29 in./73.5 cm

Yarn

Red Heart Collage, jumbo weight #7 yarn (73% acrylic, 27% wool; 58 yd./53 m per 5 oz./142 g skein)
• 9 skeins Chiffon 9985

Hook & Other Materials
• US Size P/Q (15 mm) crochet hook
• Yarn needle

Gauge
Gauge is not critical for this project.

Special Stitches
fhdc (foundation half double crochet) = Ch 2, yo and insert hook in 2nd ch from hook, yo and pull up a loop, yo and pull through 1 loop on hook (*1st ch made*), yo and pull through all loops on hook (*hdc made*), *yo and insert hook into ch of previous foundation st, yo and pull up a loop, yo and pull through 1 loop on hook (*ch made*), yo and pull through all loops on hook (*hdc made*); repeat from * until desired number of fhdc have been made.
shell = (Dc, ch 1, dc, ch 1, dc) in indicated st.

Notes
• Pattern is adjustable. For a custom size, begin with a foundation ch in any multiple of 8 + 1.
• Reserve at least 1 skein of yarn for Border section.

Instructions

Row 1: Fhdc 33, turn.

Row 2: Ch 1, sc in same, *ch 4, skip 3, sc in next; repeat from * across, turn—8 ch-4 spaces.

Row 3: Ch 4, dc in same (*counts as half-shell*), *sc in ch-4 space, ch 5**, sc in next ch-4 space, shell in next sc; repeat from * across ending last repeat at **, (dc, ch 1, dc) in last sc (*counts as half-shell*), turn—3 shells, 2 half-shells, 4 ch-5 spaces.

Row 4: Ch 1, sc in same, *shell in next sc, sc in next ch-5 space, shell in next sc, sc in middle dc of next shell; repeat from * across working last sc in 3rd ch of turning ch-4, turn—8 shells.

Row 5: Ch 5 (*counts as dc, ch-2*), *sc in middle dc of next shell, shell in next sc, sc in middle dc of next shell**, ch 5; repeat from * across ending last repeat at **, ch 2, dc in last sc, turn—3 shells, 3 ch-5 spaces, 2 ch-2 spaces.

Row 6: Ch 1, sc in same, *shell in next sc, sc in middle dc of next shell, shell in next sc, sc in next ch-5 space; repeat from * across, sc in 3rd ch of turning ch-5, turn—8 shells.

Row 7: Ch 4, dc in same (*counts as half-shell*), *sc in middle dc of next shell, ch 5, sc in middle dc of next shell**, shell in next sc; repeat from * across ending last repeat at **, (dc, ch 1, dc) in last sc (*counts as half-shell*), turn—3 shells, 2 half-shells, 4 ch-5 spaces.

Rows 8–24: Repeat Rows 4–7, ending on a repeat of Row 4.

Row 25: Ch 5 (*counts as dc, ch-2 space*), *sc in middle dc of next shell, shell in next sc, sc in middle dc of next shell**, ch 4; repeat from * across ending last repeat at **, ch 2, dc in last sc, turn—3 shells, 3 ch-4 spaces, 2 ch-2 spaces.

Continue to Border.

Border

Round 1: Ch 1, 2 hdc in 1st space, *hdc in next sc, hdc in next 3 dc, hdc in next sc**, 3 hdc in next ch-4 space; repeat from * across 1st side ending last repeat at **, (2 hdc, ch 1, 3 sc) in corner space, rotate to work into row ends, 3 sc in each ch-space across side, ch 1 at corner, sc in each st across foundation ch, ch 1 at corner, 3 sc in each ch-space across side, ch 1 at corner, sl st to 1st st to join.

Fasten off and weave in ends.

Attach fringe or tassels if desired.

Triangle Banner

Designed by Salena Baca

Chunky T-shirt yarn is on trend for home decor, and banners are always a fun way to decorate! This design can easily be made in alternate colors and yarn weights to fit your style.

Skill Level
Easy

Finished Measurements
1 triangle: 10 in./25 cm
Finished banner length: 58 in./147.5 cm

Yarn

Lion Brand Fast-Track, super bulky #6 yarn (60% cotton, 40% polyester; 149 yd./136 m per 8 oz./227 g skein)
- 1 skein Dune Buggy Denim 108 (Color A)
- 1 skein Chopper Grey 149 (Color B)

Hook & Other Materials
- US Size L-11 (8.0 mm) crochet hook
- Yarn needle

Gauge
Gauge is not critical to this project.

Instructions

Triangle (make 2 in Color A and 3 in Color B)

Make magic ring (see "Additional Resources" on page vii for link to video tutorial).

Round 1 (RS): Ch 6 (*counts as dc, ch-3 now and throughout*), [5 dc in ring, ch 3] 2 times, 4 dc in ring, sl st to top of 1st dc to join—15 dc, 3 ch-3 spaces.

Round 2: Sl st over two sts, ch 6, dc in same st, [dc in next 7 sts, (dc, ch 3, dc) in next] 2 times, dc in last 7 sts, sl st to top of 1st dc to join—27 dc, 3 ch-3 spaces.

Round 3: Sl st over two sts, ch 6, dc in same st, [dc in next 11 sts, (dc, ch 3, dc) in next] 2 times, dc in last 11 sts, sl st to top of 1st dc to join—33 dc, 3 ch-3 spaces.

Round 4: Sl st over two sts, ch 6, dc in same st, [dc in next 15 sts, (dc, ch 3, dc) in next] 2 times, dc in last 15 sts, sl st to top of 1st dc to join, fasten off—33 dc, 3 ch-3 spaces.

Join Triangles/Form Banner

Ensure triangles are facing RS, line up in join order: 1, 2, 3, 4, 5. With Color B, ch 5, beginning with triangle 5, *sc in 2nd ch of any ch-3 corner, [ch 1, skip 1 st, sc in next] 10 times, ch 1; repeat from * for remaining 4 triangles, ch 4, fasten off.

Tassels

Cut eight 10 in./25 cm pieces of yarn. Fold bundle in half evenly, loop through ch-3 space from un-worked ch-3 space of triangle, draw ends through loop, and knot to fasten.

Make 5 in Color A; attach 1 at each banner end, and 1 at each Color B triangle. Make 2 in Color B; attach 1 at each Color A triangle.

Standard Crochet Abbreviations

BL	back loop	**sc2tog**	single crochet 2 together
BLO	back loop only	**sl st**	slip stitch
BPdc	back post double crochet	**st(s)**	stitch(es)
BPhdc	back post half double crochet	**TKS**	Tunisian knit stitch
ch	chain	**TKS2tog**	Tunisian knit stitch 2 together
cl	cluster	**tr**	treble crochet
dc	double crochet	**WS**	wrong side
dc2tog	double crochet 2 together	**yo**	yarn over
fhdc	foundation half double crochet	**( )**	work instructions within parentheses into stitch or space as directed
FLO	front loop only	*****	repeat instructions following or between asterisk(s) as directed
FPdc	front post double crochet	**[ ]**	work instructions within brackets as many times as directed
FPhdc	front post half double crochet		
hdc	half double crochet		
hdc2tog	half double crochet 2 together		
M1	make 1 increase		
RS	right side		

Yarn & Materials

Craftsy
craftsy.com

Knit Picks
knitpicks.com

Lion Brand Yarns
lionbrand.com

Red Heart Yarns
RedHeart.com

Scheepjes
scheepjes.com

Acknowledgments

I would not be where I am today in the crochet world without help and support from two of my favorite colleagues and crochet idols: Danyel and Emily. Thank you both for working so tirelessly on this collection and sharing your knowledge, experience, and friendship. Many thanks are also due to my family; my love for you, and yours for me, is bliss! Finally, thanks to Stackpole Books and my wonderful friend there, Candi; you are a joy to work with, and I appreciate you!—**Salena Baca**

Salena and Emily are two of my very favorite people in the crochet world and in real life. It has been such a pleasure working and crocheting with these two amazing women. Thank you both for your encouragement and inspiration—but most of all, for your friendship! I love you both very much. I also need to thank my husband, children, and parents; they have always been supportive of my crochet career, never once complained about having to try on my designs, and have the good sense to ignore the piles of yarn stashed around the house.—**Danyel Pink**

A crochet friend is a forever friend. Danyel and Salena are my crochet friends; they have encouraged me and cheered me on for years. I have looked up to them and admired them all that time, and it is such a privilege to be included in this collection with them. Thank you both for your support, for your friendship, and for keeping it real. I'm grateful to my dear husband and children for their support through some long hours, and to my sister and sister-in-law for being my gorgeous photography models.—**Emily Truman**

Visual Index

Hats & Headbands

Alaskan Dusk Hat
page 2

Amelia Ear Warmer
page 5

City Tweed Slouch
page 8

Flower Motif Slouch
page 11

Hannah Hood
page 14

Heather Convertible Hat/Cowl
page 17

Kaleidoscope Slouch
page 21

Toasty Tunisian Head Wrap
page 24

Wraps & Other Wearables

Chroma Shawl
page 28

Diamond Twist Cowl
page 31

Dreamy Poncho
page 34

Feng Shui Wrap
page 37

Fringe Vest
page 40

Gray Skies Fingerless Mitts
page 43

Metallic Slippers
page 46

Sam Fingerless Mitts
page 49

Slightly Slipper Socks
page 52

Sparkle Soft Cowl
page 56

Sprightly Boot Cuffs
page 59

Sunburst Scarf
page 62

Bags & Totes

Bloom Market Tote
page 66

Concert Clutch
page 70

Curio Coin Purse
page 73

Fine Wine Tote
page 76

Mandala Handbag
page 79

Twisted Phone or Tablet Cozy
page 82

Kitchen & Dining

Blackberry Coffee Cozy
page 86

Hanging Herb Holder
page 89

Harbor Placemat
page 92

Hexagon Centerpiece
page 95

Hexagon Potholder
page 98

Nana's Garden Trivet
page 102

Puffy Dishcloth
page 106

Superstar Coasters
page 109

Windsor Dishcloth
page 112

Living

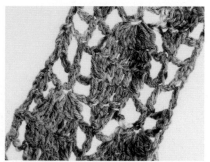

Falling Leaves Wall Tapestry
page 116

Fast-Track Basket
page 120

Fast-Track Rug
page 123

Nebula Pillow
page 126

(Sweet) Dreamcatcher
page 130

Trellis Blanket
page 133

Triangle Banner
page 136